art:
of WONDER & a WORLD

An Illustrated Alphabet, England, 18th Century

art: of WONDER & a WORLD

WRITTEN BY

JEAN MARY MORMAN

EDITORIAL CONSULTANTS:

OLIVE L. RILEY
DIRECTOR OF ART, NEW YORK CITY PUBLIC SCHOOLS

MARY COLE EMERSON
DIRECTOR OF ART, CHICAGO PUBLIC SCHOOLS

ALBERT W. PORTER
SUPERVISOR OF ART, SENIOR HIGH SCHOOLS, LOS ANGELES CITY SCHOOLS

DESIGN CONSULTANT:
NORMAN LALIBERTÉ

ART EDUCATION, INC., PUBLISHERS • BLAUVELT, NEW YORK 10913

*to
my students,
whose joyful openness
to wonder will always
expand my own.*

The Tree of Knowledge

Printed in the United States of America

Library of Congress Catalog Card Number: 67-29873

CONTENTS:

Telescope, 1877

If you live in this world, if you walk through (or around) its puddles, read its newspapers, live in its houses, move with its speed — yes, art is for you. Why? Because art is the most 'peoplish' thing people do.

Art is the difference between SEEING, and just identifying. Only people can see the shape of a puddle and the reflections it catches, the hard angles of steel girders against the sky, the light-and-dark of shadows on a stairway, the rhythm of whirling wheels at rush hour.

This is art? Almost. This is man shifting gears from the pace of everyday rush for a long look, seeing the pattern, the rhythm of rustling leaves or stark winter branches, of water dripping, of the slinking movement of a cat; *this* is man taking a long look at the things he needs, at the world rushing by, at war, at hate, at love.

And *this* is art — man responding to this LOOKING by getting NEW IDEAS, seeing his needs, seeing his world, and saying "What if . . ." "What if I design a better car . . . or a new kind of plane?" "What if I paint a picture, write a song?" Animals build by instinct; you will never see a new style sparrow's nest. Man does it the hard way — learning, looking, thinking, questioning, and coming up with an Apollo spacecraft or a unique building or a symphony . . . or a *Beanery* as Edward Kienholz did.

This is art? This is man exploring the materials of his world and developing an Apollo, recognizing the needs of its millions of people and designing a structure, transforming its sounds into a symphony, and reacting to the hollowness he sees in today's society.

KIENHOLZ The Beanery

GOYA The Prisoner in Chains

6

LOOK

—at the texture of bread, of cabbage, of bubbles in coke

—at your shadow, bending against a wall, lengthening

—at the gleam of tin cans, the color of their labels

—at the sway of grass in the wind

—at fifty more things that you SEE.

WHAT DO YOU THINK?

—Can there be beauty in your back yard?

—Are only "pretty" things art?

—Read e. e. cumming's poem *In Just Spring*. What is his idea of beauty?

—Where does art fit in the Gemini and Apollo experiments? Do you know that Massachusetts Institute of Technology and Illinois Institute of Technology require art courses of their engineering students? Why?

—The artist is the voice of his time. Compare the painting by Jean-Honoré Fragonard on page 95 (he was a court painter for France's Louis XVI) and the etching by Francisco Goya (he lived in Spain during a time of great social injustice for the poor) with Edward Kienholz's *Beanery* (done in our time). What do they tell you?

—Look at paintings by Ben Shahn and Edward Hopper (p. 104), and Marc Chagall (p. 103). What view is each one taking of our world?

Gemini XI View of India

SHAHN Mother and Child

TRY THIS

—What do you want to say about your world? About yourself? Think of a new way to say it . . . . .

just with color? with *collage?* This is a design made from many materials: magazine photos, newspaper headlines, dance bids, labels. What does your collage need?

—Can you express the sounds of your day in a visual form? Can you express its movements?

Swallow Nests

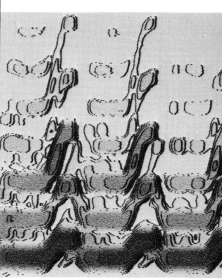

Speech Spectrogram of a Wood Thrush

7

So this is art — man making. In our "phone and charge it" age, when even do - it - yourself kits are a challenge, what has happened to art?

Two things! First, millions of people never know the thrill of getting a new idea and seeing it through, even though it is only making a cake that doesn't come in a box.

And second, we may have lost touch with the "stuff" of our world, with the wood and clay and stone — the materials men have used from cave days.

If you like to feel the wind, to dive under a wave, to walk barefoot in grass, or to make a snowman, you are close to art. If you like to cut paper into crazy patterns, or make kites, or soap box racers, you're in. If you don't, maybe you've never tried.

Student's Torn Paper Design

LOOK

—at the shape of rust on a gutter

—at the pattern of jets in the sky

—at the design of a tiger-eye marble

—at the colors in a patch of weeds.

WHAT DO YOU THINK?

—Is making things important to you? Building model cars? Making a dress? Cooking?

—Bob Dylan has a song like this: "Men make everything from toy guns that spark to flesh-colored Christs that glow in the dark. It's easy to see without looking too far that not much is really sacred." What does he mean by things being "sacred"? Someone said, "The man who does not make, destroys." What do you think? Does he mean the same kind of making that Bob Dylan speaks of?

TRY THIS

—See what you can make . . . .
> by folding and cutting paper.
> by collecting pebbles or colored glass or match sticks and making a mosaic. You might try watching water movement for an idea.
> by constructing a kite and flying it.

—Listen to music; watch a ballet on TV; sit quietly for five minutes.

PHOTOGRAPH, Ritual Room, 1965 (Detail)

KLINE New York

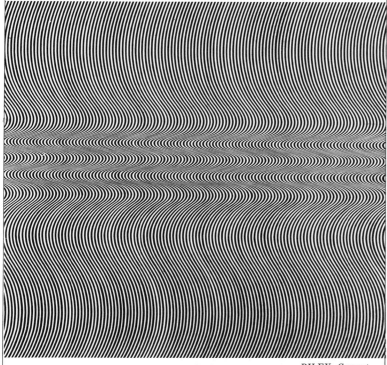

RILEY Current

Is he telling us that we have "lost touch," that we have looked at "pretty" pictures so long that we really don't SEE any more? Since the 1940's, American artists have taken a new lead in the art of the world.

Abstract Expressionist painters have forced us to a second look at colors, shapes — the things that make our sunsets and our puddles. Mark Rothko turned to color, enjoying the sensation of red next to orange, or purple next to blue. Robert Motherwell combines great slabs of color and unexpected shapes. Franz Kline cut black gashes of paint across white canvas, much as the steel girders of our high-rise constructions cut the sky.

Jackson Pollock felt the need to move with the rhythm of his whole body in his "action painting." He stood over his canvas and dripped paint in the pattern dictated by his arm and body movements.

Pop artists take their subjects right off our supermarket shelves or out of our comic strips to give us an enlarged second look. They also show us endless repetitions, papier-mâché hamburgers, old stoves. These artists also face us with the problems of our world, as Edward Kienholz did when he made his *Beanery*, with its plaster casts of people with clock heads. Marisol sets up an "all-alone-in-a-crowd" feeling with wooden block people, pasted-on faces, pinned-on dresses.

"Op" art took its name from the word optical. Do you ever look at things through a glass jar and watch them expand and contract? The Op artist designs for just such eye tricks.

With repeated stripes and shocking colors he makes forms jump and shift in our eyes—making us look again. Nature is rich with such shapes, and our man-made landscape has even more of them.

And what next? In our world of miscroscope and space flights and plastics and power, only tomorrow will tell . . . each tomorrow. The artist's language is the same. He speaks with lines and shapes and spaces and colors and textures, but what he says will always arise from what his world means to him.

LOOK

—at the shapes of shadows in photographs

—at the repeat of wire lines in a stack of shopping carts

—at the distortion of forms through glass

—at the different styles of cartoons

—at things seen through your fingers for an Op view

—at close-up views.

WHAT DO YOU THINK?

—The artist expresses his world. What was the world of the year 1200 A.D. or 1500 A.D. like? How does the spirit of the twelfth century compare with that of the fifteenth. Compare them both with our own. See pages 90-93 and 10-13.

—What new vistas have space flights and moon photos revealed to us?

—In a darkened room watch two or three stu-

MARISOL Women and Dog

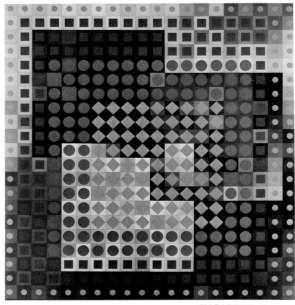

VASARELY Harmas

MOTHERWELL The Voyage

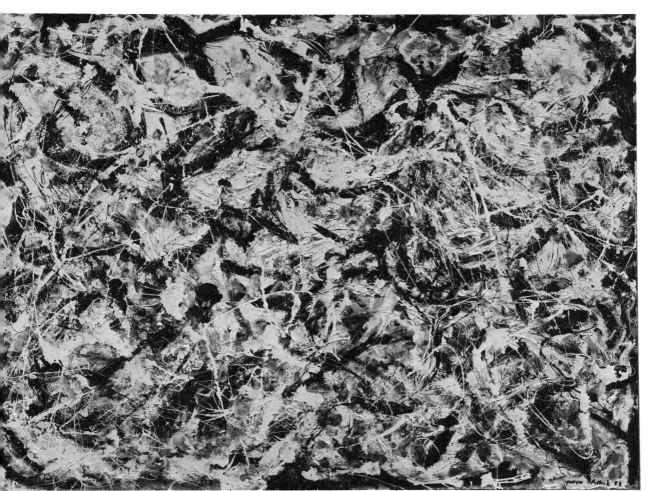

POLLOCK Grayed Rainbow

dents make line movements with flash lights. Do these movements suggest dancers? Action painting? In what way?

TRY THIS

—Use the forms you see behind a glass tumbler as the beginning of a design. What materials could catch the idea of your forms? Colored tissue in overlaid shapes? Water color on wet paper? Erased or blurred pencil drawings? What else?

—Try to get the effect of Op art with a close-up view of a section of a common object or by "expanding" a square of black paper. Cut a series of narrow shapes using all of the paper. Paste the shapes to a background with enough white space between to create a strong feeling of movement in the black and white shapes.

—Hang a frame of vertical stripes in front of your design so it can sway. Watch the shifting patterns.

—Use an overhead projector to make Op in action. Overlay and move line patterns.

—Enjoy the patterns in a kaleidoscope. Look at your world through a teleidoscope. You will see fantastic Op shapes. Try making a teleidoscope.

LICHTENSTEIN "No Thank You," 1964

13

Painters and sculptors do have a 'place in the sun' today. But what about the designers of our homes, our cars, our pots and pans? Although much good work is being done, here is a wide-open field for artists. With new materials and new ways of producing, they are thinking new.

The results? The things we use every day are not just useful, but can be well-designed, their forms growing from their functions. Compare these two telephone designs. Plastic materials and a study of how a phone is held resulted in this smooth, comfortable-to-handle shape.

Cars, airplanes, bridges, and toasters need the precision of machines for their construction. But is there still room in our mass-production world for the handmade traditional products, the hand-woven basket, the carved bowl, the blown glass? Before there were factories, everything was handmade. What are some of the differences between the factory product and the handmade product? Are some things better when manufactured and others better when handmade?

LOOK

—for art in the things you use

—for design that *is* structure in skyscrapers

—for design in department store window displays

—for good product design in packaging

—for the "line" of a car.

WHAT DO YOU THINK?

—What is meant by the functional design of a car, ice skates, a camera?

—What shapes can plastics take? What functions can they serve?

—Name new and traditional architectural materials. What advantages do new materials offer over the old?

—What handcrafts are still important today? Find out more about one of them. Do you know any craftsmen — potters, weavers, jewelry makers, carpenters?

—Compare old and new styles of furniture. In what ways does each style reflect the time in which it was designed?

TRY THIS

—Design your own. If you could make a car, a set of dishes, or a lamp, how would you plan it for function and style?

—Look into stitchery, weaving, basketry, ceramics, rug hooking, papier-mâché, jewelry, leather. Which would you work in?

—Design a package for any manufactured product. What kind of lettering and what kind of coloring would suit it? Find examples of good package design.

VOULKOS Ceramic

CONTEMPORARY AFRICAN Woven Figures

Racing Cars

WHAT'S IN A MATERIAL? :5

What happens when an artist and his material get together? There was a time when the artist, controlling his material, worked his paint into the appearance of satin or hair or grass, polished his marble to look like skin. Today the action works both ways: the material "speaks" and the artist works in response to the essential character of his oils or water color, his clay or granite or steel. The artist feels strongly about this, about his own honesty in the use of his materials.

Each material has its own personality. Steel is thin, strong, flexible. It can be welded, hammered, bent. Stone is heavy, solid. Wood can be carved in its log shape; it can be sawed into boards or delicately cut with a jigsaw. Clay is pliable, but can be hardened in a kiln.

Water color is transparent, thin; tempera and oils are usually opaque, thick. Each has its own "voice", much as a trombone and a guitar have their own qualities.

Today many artists deliberately choose non-traditional materials. In addition to new industrial products, "thrown-away" objects are often used.

LOOK

—at the finger impressions in a wheel-thrown pot

—at the gouge marks on a wood carving

—at the grain in wood

—at the shapes in scrap auto parts.

GABO   Linear Construction in Space, No. 4

NOGUCHI   Bird C (Mu)

ROSZAK   Sea Sentinel

WHAT DO YOU THINK?

—Compare this detail of a Flemish Renaissance painting with the painting by Georges Rouault. Both are oil paintings; both are good methods of using oil.

—What is the difference in appearance between these oil paintings and John Marin's water-color?

—Listen to records to discover the special 'voice' of a trumpet, sax, tuba, guitar. Can you match each with a painting or sculptural material?

—Compare the photos of sculpture. Look at other actual pieces of sculpture in museums or parks. How does material affect the form of sculpture?

TRY THIS

—Find scrap boards with a strong grain. Make crayon rubbings on paper pressed over them, or ink them with a brayer and make a print of their patterns.

—Experiment with water color to see how you can lighten and darken colors; suggest textures with a brush (or what other ways?); get a wet or dry effect.

—Use materials that are available to you in a way that emphasizes their particular qualities.

VAN EYCK Altarpiece (Detail)   ROUAULT Christ Mocked by Soldiers

MARIN Boat Off Deer Isle

Do you take a "what-is-it?" approach to painting or sculpture? Do you look only to identify the trees, or the man, or the sailboat? This is like trying to swim without getting wet, or eating without tasting. You miss the real flavor.

The artist is the man who sees — sees the riot of color in a garden as well as the ugly problems of our world. The artist is never content to say with his paint "This is a red barn." He gets into his subject, or simply into his paint or stone, and says something personal.

The arts — all of them — have their own language. Poets get their ideas across with figures of speech, even with the very sounds of their words. Read aloud these lines from *Velvet Shoes* by Elinor Wylie and listen to the softness of the sounds. Which consonants give this effect? Which vowel sounds are most used?

> *"Let us walk in the white*
> *   snow*
> *In a soundless space*
> *With footsteps quiet and*
> *   slow.*
> *I shall go shod in silk*
> *And you in wool,*
> *White as a white cow's*
> *   milk,*
> *More beautiful than the*
> *   breast of a gull"*

Contrast it to this, from *Night Journey* by Theodore Roethke.

> *"My muscles move with*
> *   steel,*
> *I wake in every nerve.*
> *I watch a beacon swing*
> *From dark to blazing*
> *   bright;*
> *We thunder through*
> *   ravines*
> *And gullies washed*
> *   with light."*

DAVIS The Paris Bit

PICASSO Three Musicians

Musicians say it with pitch, with chords that blend or with harsh-sounding (dissonant) chords, with loudness or softness. Listen to *Sorcerer's Apprentice* by Paul Dukas, or *Grand Canyon Suite* by Ferde Grofé. Also, listen to Claude Débussy's three nocturnes for orchestra: *Nuages, Fetes, Sirenes*. What others can you find?

Dancers use the movements of their bodies to interpret their themes. Oriental dancers use even finger movements.

Painters and sculptors "talk" with line, shape, form, color, texture, space. Each of these art elements opens as many possibilities as there are artists who work with them.

FEININGER Mellinge

TOBEY   New York Tablet

LOOK

—for figures of speech that give a stronger idea of strength, a colder idea of cold

—for a loud blue, a cold blue, a mysterious blue, a warm blue.

LISTEN

—to the sounds of your day: voices, transportation sounds, TV; what other?

—to sounds of nature.

—to different kinds of music. Try to get the mood or idea of each one.

WHAT DO YOU THINK?

—In *Three Musicians* Picasso is certainly not telling you what they look like. Why did he paint them in this way? What ideas do his shapes and colors suggest?

—Compare these different ideas of a city to those by John Marin (p. 52), Piet Mondrian (p. 53), and Fernand Léger (p. 35).

TRY THIS

—Find colors or sections of type from a magazine that match the sound of your day. Make a collage expressing it.

—What is your idea of a city? How can you use the artist's language to express it?

—Draw your own home environment—kitchen, closets, garage, etc. Make your drawings express those things that are important to you.

All the creative and performing arts have their own languages. But one thing belongs to all of them, just as it belongs to us, to our heart beat, our walk, our breathing. This one thing is *rhythm!* What is rhythm? We can both hear and see rhythm. What makes a march rhythm, a jazz rhythm, a waltz rhythm? Waves lap up to the shore in a rhythm, sometimes calm, sometimes stormy. Poetry has rhythm.

Is it just continuous movement? Tap your finger evenly. Then tap a march beat. You have two things: repetition and emphasis.

Every art has these qualities of rhythm. It is what brings us in, carries us through a song, or a painting, or a poem. It is what makes flowing water or birds in flight, or the pattern of a plowed field fascinating.

How does the painter or sculptor, the weaver or potter, bring rhythm into his work? By repeating his lines, shapes, colors, movements; by making them larger or smaller, brighter or duller. In these city scenes, each artist has set a different rhythm, a different emphasis. Compare them.

There is a rhythm of life in a big city or a little town. The rhythm of life in Europe, or in the mountains of Peru, or the South Sea Islands, is different from the U. S. A. The rhythm of life right here 100 years ago was very different from that of today. Do these different rhythms get into the art of these places and times?

STEICHEN George Washington Bridge

WOOD American Gothic

MANESSIER Rowboats

STELLA Gran Cairo

LOOK

—for repetition in fences, lamp posts, spokes of a wheel, bricks in a wall

—at the rhythm of birds' wings, or a football formation

—for the shadow rhythm of one building's forms reflected in the windows of another building

—for the rhythm of moving wheels.

MARSH Tattoo and Haircut

LISTEN

—to your own breathing. Does it change when you run or get excited?

—to gym class doing exercises

—to the rhythm of cars going by at rush hour

—to a train moving at a fast clip

—to cars on a wet street.

WHAT DO YOU THINK?

—What tempo of life do you find in Grant Wood's *American Gothic*, Frank Stella's *Gran Cairo*, Reginald Marsh's *Tattoo & Haircut*, Edward Steichen's *George Washington Bridge*?

—What is the difference in rhythm between Alfred Manessier's *Rowboats* and Wassily Kandinsky's *Improvization* (p. 51). How did each painter achieve his rhythm? Can you find music that has similar rhythms?

—Look through your Folio of the history of art on pages 80 to 108 to see the variety of rhythms that catch the pace of each period.

TRY THIS

—Use one simple shape, such as a square or triangle, or one simple line movement and with chalk repeat it many times. Vary its color and size for emphasis. Describe the rhythm you have set up.

—Try to interpret the rhythm of a musical composition in paint, or in a 3-D wire form. Don't just "keep time" in your work. Catch the kind of rhythm by expressing it in the space that moves over the entire dimensions of your paper.

—Find examples of the rhythm of moving forms as the Futurists painted them. Compare a futurist painting (see one by Balla on page 39) with multiple exposure in photography. Can you express rush hour, or dismissal time, or a dance in this way?

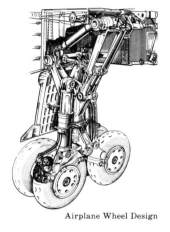

Airplane Wheel Design

Take a pencil, a pen, a stick, a brush—whatever your tool, you make lines. Put together Tool & Artist & Idea and you will get new lines, unique lines every time.

Lines can define objects, like mountain or mouse. They can also express ideas like action, joy, hatred, peace. Their personality comes out in their Quality and Direction.

The Quality of a line is its thinness or thickness, its roughness or smoothness. Each kind of tool makes its own kind of line. Lines can be flimsy or forceful, elegant or crude. They can be clumsy, graceful, confused, sorrowful, gay, serious, giddy.

Line quality grows from the idea the artist wants to express. Lines used to show factory workers would be different from lines showing dancers. Even *factory* can be said in any number of ways. A scribbled line can catch rugged strength and activity. In contrast, repeated smooth lines build up ideas of immensity and precision of machines.

Direction can make lines majestic, weary, or really swinging. Diagonals speak action; curves are rhythmic; horizontals are as quiet as sleep.

Lines can move into the picture and create a three-dimensional effect, or they can divide the surface and become a flat two-dimensional design.

LOOK

—for the lines in railroad tracks, in different kinds of trees

—for lines of telephone poles and wires against the sky

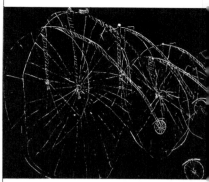

Child's Drawing

KOLLWITZ Mother and Child

REMBRANDT
Entombment of Christ (Detail)

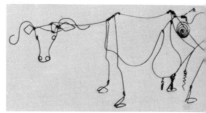

CALDER Cow

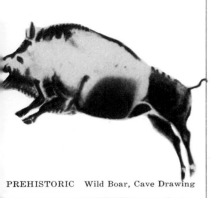

PREHISTORIC   Wild Boar, Cave Drawing

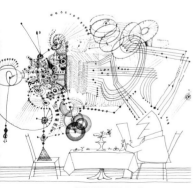

VAN GOGH   Cypresses

STEINBERG   Conversation

LALIBERTÉ   Sketch

—for fold lines in paper, cloth, plastic

—for lines in faces— lines of sorrow, of age, of strength, of laughter

—for lines of cracks, of weathered wood or paint

—for lines in a dandelion pod.

WHAT DO YOU THINK?

—Compare the line of this prehistoric boar with Diego Rivera's lines of laborers in his *Sleep*. Quality? Direction? Find other examples of interesting line movements in the work of Kathe Kollwitz, Paul Klee, and other artists.

—In some periods of art, lines were used as outline and pattern and expression. In other periods, all edges were blended into a 3-D effect. Contrast the Catalan Madonna (p. 73) with a Renaissance Madonna and Child (p. 36).

—What effect can quality and direction of line have in clothes? In furniture? In architecture? In automobiles and airplanes?

—Look for line quality in various types of sculpture: flowing, dynamic, strong, graceful.

—Steel rods can be welded together (see Roszak's *Sea Sentinel* on p. 16), or simply left to vibrate. Continuous lines of wire can make a charging horse.

TRY THIS

—Use a quick *scribble* line to catch the gesture of a baseball pitcher, a dancer, a high jumper. Work inside the shapes instead of outlining them. Make them heavier where the weight or force is.

—Do *contour* line drawings of people, chairs, purses. Follow each edge slowly, "feeling" it with your eyes. Look at the model rather than at your paper, drawing without breaking your line.

—Look at a Rembrandt etching. Notice how he builds up shadows with many lines. Draw bottles with many lines but no outlines. Look for lights and shadows on them. Try long lines or lines as short as dots.

—Use sticks or wire or tooth picks to make a three-dimensional animal.

—Use string to make a continuous line design.

—Experiment with different tools to get as many linear qualities as you can. What can you express with each of them?

LALIBERTÉ   Drawing

25

GERMAN Woodcut

REMBRANDT Etching (Detail)

DURER Etching (Detail)

NOLDE The Doctors (Woodcut)

ORIENTAL HOKUSAI, Tuning The Samisen (Woodcut)

Some artists' materials belong to line like waves to an ocean. Woodblock (or linoleum) print is one of these. The very gouges used to cut the design into the block make lines and leave lines between cuts. The surface of the block is inked, and the final design printed on paper.

In the first days of the printing press (1527), woodblock designs were cut to look like pen sketches. Gradually artists let the block speak for itself. Today the lines of the wood as well as the gouge are important.

Woodblock prints were started in Japan in the late 18th century as the "poor man's art". Japanese people have a deep love of art and beauty; woodblock prints made art available at lower costs so all could enjoy them.

Etching is another graphic, "copy-making" process that is carried out in line, but it works in exact reverse of block printing. Lines are drawn into a wax-coated and smoked copper plate. With its back and sides protected, the plate is placed in acid so that these lines will be eaten or etched into the plate. Ink is applied to an etching, not on the surface as in a woodcut, but into the grooves. The surface is cleaned, the plate is run through a press, and the paper print picks up only the many fine lines.

Rembrandt was a master of etching. Study this detail as an example of his technique.

Another graphic art is serigraphy (silk screen printing). A design is made by blocking out lines or shapes on silk, and then pressing paint with a squeegee through the silk stretched tightly on a wooden frame.

LOOK

—for boards that you can use for wood block — apple crate ends, ripped pieces, old ones

—for materials that can be glued to boards and printed — net, burlap, cord, string

—for more wood block prints and etchings.

WHAT DO YOU THINK?

—*Graphic* processes are methods of making many copies of a print. Before the printing press was invented, wood blocks were used to cut pages of letter forms. Look into the Gutenberg invention to see how it revolutionized printing.

—Compare the Japanese style of woodcut with the Western style. Notice the absence of shadows on faces in Japanese designs. For them, dark areas on faces are "unrealistic". Contrast this with Rembrandt's *chiaroscuro* technique (Italian word for strong accents of light and shadow).

TRY THIS

—Make a block print from wood or linoleum. Use materials glued to boards or to cardboard as a means of providing an underlay color.

—Do an etching by scratching lines on a piece of acetate. Apply ink by rubbing it into the grooves. You will need a roller press for pressure to print.

—Think of other ways that you can print. Carve a design in an eraser or potato and print it as a repeat pattern.

SISTER CORITA   Greek Proverb (Serigraph)

KOHN   Tiger (Woodcut)

MONET
Waterlilies

TURNER
Valley of Aosta

SEURAT
La Grand Jatte

Giving the title COLOR to this page is like setting a child in the middle of a toyland—there are so many fascinating ways to go that you don't know where to begin.

Color is light. Color is pigment. Color is screaming circus fun and grey death. Colors are as alive as electricity.

Color is light. For centuries, artists painted blue skies, green grass, dark shadows. Then came the Impressionists, in the late 1870's, painting outdoors in the morning mist, dismal fog, or glow of sunset, and claiming that whatever we see changes color in these various atmospheres and times of day. Claude Monet painted the Rouen cathedral in France many times and each painting has quite varied color effects.

Physicists, experimenting with varying wave lengths of light, were developing the science of color at this same time. Bending light rays through a prism, they demonstrated that all colors are contained in the white light of sunlight, and they showed too that our own eye blends and responds to color.

Look hard at something red for a few moments. Look away to a white surface and you will see green. This complement (*completing* color) contains all the light rays that red absorbs. Used together, these two complements are strong accents. *Mixed* together they "eat each other up", producing grey. Make a pin wheel: half red, half green. Spin it. Try this same experiment with yellow and violet, with blue and orange.

Impressionists, using these theories, began paint-ing dabs of pure colors next to each other instead of blending them. Red and yellow dabs made a sparkling orange; red and green intensified each other; in even quantities they became, in the viewer's eye, rich shadow area. The artificial black shadows of past styles were eliminated.

Georges Seurat took the next step, *Neo-Impressionism,* and worked this method into a science, measuring proportions of colors to be combined, and applying his paint in careful dots. His method is called *pointillism.* See his *Sunday Afternoon on the Island of La Grande Jatte.*

LOOK

—at all the variations of one color as daylight shines on your sweater or your shirt

—at the same color in fluorescent and incandescent light

—at red through green glass

—at rainbows, or colors in an oily puddle

—at the color of morning, of rain, of dusk

—at mist around street lights.

WHAT DO YOU THINK?

—Listen to music by Debussy, an Impressionist composer; compare his effects with Claude Monet's paintings.

—Painters of the Renaissance used *chiaroscuro* (light and dark). Compare the light in the painting, *View of Toledo,* by El Greco (p. 52) to the Impressionists' light.

—Today the field of color and light is wide-open to the artist. New means of projecting scenery are revolutionizing theatre sets. Even computer-programmed patterns become the artist's medium. Look up the newest information in these fields, and see Chryssa's neon design *Analysis of the Letter B,* reflecting and repeating on all sides of its glass case (p. 59).

—Look at Joseph Turner's painting, *The Valley of Aosta: Snowstorm, Avalanche and Thunderstorm.* Although he was many years ahead of the Impressionists, he looked for the same atmospheric effects of light.

—Look at movies with light in mind. How can the producer use it for composition and for expression?

—Your TV picture actually comes through as lines. What can you find out about the scientific principles of TV transmission?

TRY THIS

—Use projectors — slide or overhead — to experiment with transparent and translucent materials. Blend, intensify or dull colors with other colors.

—Overlay colored tissues, then glue down with starch or shellac.

—If you are interested in photography, try to capture atmospheric effects.

—Look for strong chiaroscuro in nature's shadows, in controlled lighting.

Fortunately for us, even prehistoric man saw colors in the earth — yellow-ochre and red-brown of clay, black of charred wood, white of lime. With that human "what if," he first rubbed these pigments on cave walls, then learned to mix them with animal fat to make them stay. And there painting began.

Since then, man has used every kind of substance to make color — all the colors of the rainbow and variations of them. Plants (like indigo), berries, sea shells, minerals — all these have been used for pigments. Today most pigments are synthetic (chemically produced).

The painter blends, relates, contrasts colors. Although many theories have been presented for color relationships, three colors — red, yellow, blue — are still most used as the primary, or basic colors which contain all others. From these primaries, all other colors can be mixed. Mixing primaries in paint produces orange (red and yellow), green (blue and yellow), and violet (blue and red). In the light spectrum these same colors stand out as "pure"—*Red*, orange, *Yellow*, green, *Blue*, violet with between colors being a blend of each neighboring color.

But just as light conditions "tone down" the color of your sweater or of a wall, so the painter controls the quality of these pure colors. Adding white or black produces light or dark variations that still may be brilliant, such as a candy pink or rich wine color.

To soften or dull a color, the painter adds the opposite or complementary color, the one which contains everything except that color.

LOOK

—at colors that have weathered

—at all the reds in an apple, at all the greens in leaves

—at the colors of fruit and vegetables in a store

WHAT DO YOU THINK?

—How do colors affect other colors? Experiment with squares of color mounted on white, black, complementary color . . . Do the squares appear to change in size, to change in brilliance?

—Can colors be crisp, hot, cool, heavy, light, sour?

TRY THIS

—Using only two primary colors with black and white, do an abstract painting. Try to mix as many variations as possible; try to make color shapes move forward, move behind; make them carry your eye through the painting. Overlay colors with dry brush or other methods. Have a class critique.

—Try using two complements and white. Compare the effect of this with the results of your first painting.

—Collect as many small swatches as you can of any one color, using magazine photos, actual material, etc.

—Full-color reproductions in magazines and books are produced from red, yellow, blue, and black inked plates. Ask a printer to show you color separation plates.

We often speak of red as hot and blue as cold. But it is when colors get together that the action begins. Colors can set moods — harmony, sadness, wild excitement, mystery. Any colors can be combined; the purpose, idea, effect, suggest which to choose and how to "tone" them. In paintings the artist may work to make colors advance or recede. He may focus on a form with a brilliant color, or he may combine colors so intense that they make your eyes jump, like Ellsworth Kelly and other "hard edge" painters. See his *Red, Green, Blue* on page 58.

Following after the Impressionists' new approaches to color, artists took many directions. Post-Impressionist Paul Cézanne began using color to build solid forms, stroke by stroke.

Another Post-Impressionist, Vincent Van Gogh, made color vibrate with emotion, using it to get the mood he wanted. Do you enjoy the fire of his *Sunflowers* against their powerful blue background? (p. 62)

In the early 1900's, a group of German painters, known as Expressionists, exaggerated form and color to express an idea or an emotion. Emile Nolde shows character and suffering in faces. Wassily Kandinsky began working with color, form, and movement in purely abstract forms, often relating them to music.

Paul Klee's paintings are often considered childlike. Look at his *Puppet Show* on page 49.

Henri Matisse led a group of artists called the Fauves or "wild beasts." They used bold, flat color in astounding combinations that remind us of the Persian miniatures of centuries before. See pp. 54-55.

LOOK

—for color in advertisements and magazine illustrations

—for colors that harmonize

—for colors that clash

—for new color patterns in clothes

—for outdoor color when it is sunny; later at the same color when it is overcast.

—Look for the writer's way of using color to reinforce an emotional impact.

LISTEN

—to music for its "color".

WHAT DO YOU THINK?

—Color in your home or your clothes can be expressive. Would colors for a game room be suitable for a kitchen?

—What factors should enter into planning colors for a room?

—Many painters today use closely related colors like pink, orange, and red together. Today's music follows the same trend toward *dissonance* rather than easily blending harmony. Listen to works by Igor Stravinsky or Modest Mussorgsky or Aaron Copland.

TRY THIS

—Do a painting using colors you think you will not like together. **Try bright, bold colors;** dull, mysterious colors. Discuss class results.

—Do a self-portrait in expressionistic color.

—Interpret a musical work in color.

The distinct country of your eyes, gifted with green twilight e.e. cummings

The dusk of firs and shining white birches Karen Peyton

Fluxions of yellow and dusk on the waters Make a wide, dreaming pansy of an old pond in the night Carl Sandburg

Where the sea meets the moon-blanched sand Mathew Arnold

ALBRIGHT   That Which I Should Have Done I Did Not Do, 1931-1941

Art has been defined as "the celebration of the ordinary." The artist is alive to *things* — to the roughness of brick, the fluff of clouds, the scratch of sandpaper, and the slick of satin.

And he is aware that we feel with our eyes as well as our fingers. In painting, sculpture, architecture, in crafts, such as weaving and pottery, artists make use of texture to give their forms this feel, both to the touch and to the eye.

Painters approach texture in widely different ways. One way is to simulate (or to appear to be) a kind of texture. Sir Thomas Lawrence simulated satin in this portrait of Mrs. Jens Wolff. The English society painters of the 18th century delighted in this. Some of today's artists use this technique. Ivan Albright's paintings have a morbid realism of flabby skin and decaying wood. Andrew Wyeth's meticulous egg-temperas catch dry grass and blowing curtains with remarkable sensitivity.

Surrealism uses simulated textures, creating real-imaginary things like Salvador Dali's melting watches in his *Persistence of Memory* (p. 103).

Sculpture, too, has its simulated textures. Greek sculptors made marble look like flesh. Late 18th century marble portraits even imitated lace.

Today's painters and sculptors are more interested in the texture of their material — the paint itself, the palette knife, or brush stroke, the grain of wood, the tool marks in stone.

Architecture went through a period of artificial textures. During the Victorian era of the late 19th century, plaster columns were painted to look like marble, and fussy decorations were added to walls. Today the beauty of real textures — stone, wood, concrete, metal — makes many of our modern buildings pleasing to the eye.

LOOK

—at textures in the sky and on the ground

—at the textures of a woven basket

—at feathers, shells, driftwood, seed pods

—at the differences in wood grains.

FEEL

—the smoothness of an apple, of silk, of glass

—the dryness of a potato skin, of popcorn, of burlap

—the roughness of tree bark, of woolen cloth

—the softness of bread, of velvet, of foam rubber.

WHAT DO YOU THINK?

—Compare examples of simulated texture. Look up information about Surrealism and also Flemish Renaissance paintings. Do these paintings show the same *purpose* of imitating the textures of nature as the Albright and Wyeth paintings show?

—Compare a 19th Century Victorian house with one of modern style. How is each one "decorated"?

—Study your own painting experiments for the textures you made with your tools, with overlay of colors, with wet or dry paint.

ROUAULT A Clown

LAWRENCE Mrs. Jens Wolff

Victorian House

WYETH, A. Ground Hog Day

GREEK Head of Athena

—Textures in sculpture come from the material. Stone chips off, leaving a rough granular surface. Wood is cut with a gouge, leaving smooth grooves. Clay responds to every pressure of a tool or finger. Look at examples of these and other materials. Compare them.

—Do musical instruments have "textured" sounds? The saxaphone? The oboe? The harp? Listen to recordings of instruments and give each one a texture.

—Look for the use of texture in photography.

TRY THIS

—With crayon or soft pencil, make rubbings of a variety of surfaces you find on the way home and in your home. Place thin paper on the surface and rub over it with crayon. Make a design of all these textures.

—Do a Surrealist collage. Cut apples, faces, bottles, etc., from photographed textures of other things.

—Experiment with clay. Texture the surface by pressing found objects into it in repeated patterns.

—Making a monoprint is an exciting approach to painting. Paint on glass, then press your paper to the surface. Build up colors, forms, textures, layer on layer. Think of different ways of monoprinting.

—Experiment with many kinds of materials — cardboard, match sticks, tooth picks, seeds. Combine them on a flat surface. Or make a 3-D cardboard design and add textures.

—Use the waxiness of crayon in as many textural ways as you can. Scratch into it, paint over it, melt it. What else?

—Weave on a cardboard loom, including metal baling strips, straw, reeds, wood veneer within the yarn design.

—Be sure to strive for good design in the activities above.

The artist's *"tree"* will never grow; his *"man"* will never breathe. No matter how realistic his style, or how far from it, the artist is not making people or trees. As the musician makes sounds, the artist makes shapes and forms, and often he finds them fascinating enough in themselves without representing anything.

Why? Because shapes and forms and lines and colors can say much more than just "a tiger" or "a house". The Chinese say that in order to paint a tiger you must feel like a tiger. The shape, then, expresses not just the stripes, but the ferocity of the animal.

You do the same thing with your voice as you speak words. Say "hello" in many different tones. It can be friendly or bitter or timid or unhappy.

The artist does this with his subjects. Charles Burchfield, an American watercolorist, painted a summer landscape with heat-full shapes in his *Summer Afternoon*. Vincent Van Gogh portrayed cypresses of France in shapes that seem to be writhing in agony (p. 25), while Fernand Léger builds a mechanical *City*. Joan Miró uses fantasy shapes in his *Carnival of Harlequin*.

MIRO Carnival of Harlequin
LEGER The City, 1919
BRUEGHEL, P. The Wedding Dance

BURCHFIELD Summer Afternoon

DA VINCI Madonna and Child

LOOK

—at the shapes of pots and pans, knives and forks

—at the tread on a tire or on your shoes

—at the sparkling, broken shapes of grape jelly on your bread

—at the shapes of clouds

—at the shapes of pottery

—at the shapes of ice cubes in a glass of water

—at the static shapes on your TV screen.

WHAT DO YOU THINK?

—Compare these two woodblock prints of Japanese dancers. How does the shape express the dance?

—In Pieter Breughel's *Wedding Dance* you see the roundness of jolly Flemish peasants. In Leonardo da Vinci's *Madonna and Child with St. Anne and St. John* round forms also predominate. Do these round forms have the same character? Compare both paintings to Picasso's *Mother and Child.*

—Use a microscope to watch amoeba movement, to study the shapes of crystals. Look at a piece of copper wire in a drop of silver nitrate. Watch the crystals form. Find many other things to view — feathers, oil, etc. Compare these shapes to large ones that you see around you.

—The shapes of furniture help to give a room its personality. Find photos of modern rooms and period styles. Compare them. Notice the color schemes and color tones. Do they belong to the style? Why, or why not?

—Writing is often analyzed to reveal character. Look at the differences in your handwriting and that of your friends. Compare American writing with typical European styles, with the brush stroke shapes of Oriental letters, with the broad-stroke lettering of medieval manuscripts, with many different script styles in advertising.

TRY THIS

—Take apart an old motor. Draw its parts — or make a construction with them.

—Use small rocks as models and draw them to look like huge boulders and mountains.

—Look at your hand from different views. Do a large contour drawing of it. Turn it into an abstraction with colors that fit its shapes.

—What kind of shape is right for clay? What shapes are functional for a cup, a pitcher, a dish? Make one of these; or maybe your piece will create its own function. Make a new form for a thing-through-which-to-view-the-world.

—Experiment with hair styles on round, oval, pointed, square-jawed face shapes. Draw the shapes and try several styles for each. Evaluate them.

PICASSO Mother and Child by the Sea

ORIENTAL Japanese Dancers

Shapes tend that way too — to belong together. Look back at the paintings you have seen. There is character in El Greco's shapes — you find it in his backgrounds just as much as in his figures. Like flames, his shapes taper, expand, curve in and out. (p. 52 and 95)

Lyonel Feininger's shapes are almost always straight-edged diagonals, forming misty overlays. Diego Rivera fills his picture *Sleep* with heavy curves to express weariness.

Piet Mondrian's paintings are based on clear-cut rectangular shapes that divide his canvas into squares and rectangles. (p. 53)

Just as in music you can often hear two or more kinds of sounds working together — like the flow of the sax and the beat of drums, or the effect of a whole orchestra — paintings often interweave different kinds of shapes. Sometimes their very belonging together comes from their sharp contrasts.

The painter orchestrates, or works together his shapes and colors with opposition or harmony. Look at the "hard-edge" painting by Ellsworth Kelly on page 58. Notice how he "floats" his colors against the color background.

This orchestration can be static, a "standing still" effect, or dynamic, a lively and moving effect. Horizontal and vertical shapes are usually static. Curved and diagonal shapes are usually dynamic.

MONDRIAN Farm at Duivendrecht

MONDRIAN Trees

LOOK

—through a cardboard finder to frame compositions of odd shapes to be found in your neighborhood. Make some drawings of them

—at the layout of a newspaper page

—at the difference in shapes of buildings.

WHAT DO YOU THINK?

—Piet Mondrian did not always draw just rectangles. This farm scene is one of his earliest paintings. His *Trees* is a further step toward abstraction. His style of painting is called *Purism.* He tried to eliminate everything extra. How is his approach being used today in the useful arts, such as furniture design, dress, interior design, advertising? Find examples.

—Look at the pattern of kimonos in the Japanese painting *No Robes on Lacquered Racks.* What unifies these different shapes? The Futurists were a group of painters who tried to show the shape of motion. Compare Giacomo Balla's *Swifts: Paths of Movement & Dynamic Sequences* with a multiple exposure photo. What possibilities does photography have for expressing motion?

—Look for relation of shapes in photographs of room furnishings.

ORIENTAL Japanese Painting "No Robes On Lacquered Racks"

RIVERA Sleep

BALLA Swifts: Paths of Movement & Dynamic Sequences

TRY THIS

—Compose a design with newspaper headline letters. Cut them in half; invert some; cut up the letter; design only with the curved and straight-edged shapes.

—Some hard-edge painters try to relate their shapes to make foreground and background interchangeable. Use cut paper or paint to make a design in this manner.

—Cut two identical sets of shapes. Make a design from each set, trying to get two very different impacts. Color can help achieve this.

—Look at a group of bottles or rocks or people and draw the spaces around them (called negative shapes).

—Cut a photograph into strips and shift them to suggest motion.

—Project shapes of bolts, nuts, glass jars, cut shapes — many things — on an overhead projector. Arrange, relate the forms.

CEZANNE Still Life with Ginger Jar and Eggplants

It all started with Paul Cézanne, known as the Father of Modern Art. Using his brush strokes like bricks, he built his landscapes into simple, solid forms. "Everything in nature" he said, "can be reduced to a sphere or cylinder or cone or cube."

And there it was for "what-if" thinkers like Picasso and Braque to pick up. They began *Cubism*. Their first works were studies of planes, like this *Head of a Woman* by Pablo Picasso. But soon they began flattening their paintings and devising new ways of relating shapes.

Here are some of their new ways:

1. MULTIPLE VIEWS — We can see things from many views; the artist can combine these views, showing both the front and the profile of a face, or the top and front of a vase.

2. TRANSPARENCY— When one object is behind another, the full shape of both can be drawn, making a new shape as they overlap.

3. MARRIAGE OF CONTOURS—The right edge of one form becomes the left edge of another.

4. PROJECTION—A movement begins, is interrupted by another, and continues farther on.

5. SHIFTING PLANES — For interest and composition, the artist "bends" a movement.

6. PART FOR WHOLE — He might also cut through a shape and leave half or move half.

The Cubists' interest in the geometry of a face sent them to the museums for a new look at African masks and ancestor statues. Here was the same strong sense of design that the Cubists were seeking. Each African tribe has its own characteristic style—some oval, some angular, some round, but all rhythmic designs.

LOOK

—at the cubes and cones and cylinders in a supermarket

BRAQUE Man With A Guitar

PICASSO Head of a Woman

AFRICAN Mask

PICASSO Weeping Woman

—at a carton of eggs

—at a drinking glass from every angle

—through glass bottles at more bottles.

WHAT DO YOU THINK?

—Look at Cézanne's *Still Life with Ginger Jar and Eggplants*. It looks realistic, but he has distorted the bowl in order to show the round top and the full side at the same time. Find repetitions of this round shape. What other shape does he weave into this picture?

—The Cubists made still life an adventure. Look for their devices in Braque's *Still Life: Le Jour*. (p. 61)

—The Cubists, especially Picasso, soon began to go beyond the geometric style. Look at his *Weeping Woman*.

TRY THIS

—Look at more examples of African sculpture. Try designing a mask portrait of a person you know. Stylize hair, features, etc. Use cut and folded paper, basket reed, or wire and papier-mâché.

—Use some or all of the Cubists' devices to make your own still life. Have someone pose playing a guitar. Let your design catch the rhythm of the music.

—Pile up boxes at many angles. Using black, gray, and white paper, cut shapes to show planes. Include light, medium, and dark colors in one color family.

ORIENTAL Chinese Calligraphy

ROMANESQUE Christ in Glory

We do it with our voice, with our words, with our gestures. To describe the game you won, the show you like or don't like, you exaggerate. A look can be so strong that it needs no words.

The poet does this with figures of speech.

Elizabeth Bishop describes "The Fish":

Here and there his brown skin hung in strips like ancient wallpaper. . . .

And Carl Sandburg calls "Chicago"

a tall bold slugger set vivid against the little soft cities; fierce as a dog with tongue lapping for action, cunning as a savage pitted against the wilderness. . . .

From Elinor Wylie's "Pretty Words"

I love smooth words, like gold-enameled fish. . . .

From e. e. cummings —

And there's the moon, thinner than a watch spring

In the street of the sky night walks scattering poems.

Spring is like a perhaps hand. . . .

When the artist exaggerates his shapes and colors, we call this *Expressionism.* Picasso combined *cubistic* and *expressionistic* shape in his *First Steps.* The mother becomes a protective arc, and the baby's uncertain feet and his excited face are twisted and distorted.

This isn't new. Painters in the 10th century were doing it. In this fresco, *Christ in Glory,* from a Romanesque church, the curved shapes express the idea of power, infinity, glory.

Picasso protests the wartime massacre in the town of Guernica through intense exaggeration. Marc Chagall sings of his love through forms and colors that float in air. (p. 103)

In Chinese calligraphy (writing), one character stands for an idea rather than a letter. It is hard to translate into English because, for example, the character for man can mean a great man or a crafty man in accordance with the shading of the brush strokes.

PICASSO First Steps

WATCH

—hand gestures

—facial expressions

—excited movements

—nervous movements.

LISTEN

—to tone-of-voice descriptions

—to the pitch of an excited voice

—to the sounds of a basketball game

—to the sounds of a department store

—to the sound of quiet

—to *Sounds of Silence* by Simon and Garfunkel.

PICASSO *Guernica*

WHAT DO YOU THINK?

—Study Picasso's *Guernica*. Can you find the shape of a scream? This painting is carried out in gray, black and white. What does this add to the idea? Notice the strong diagonal movements through *Guernica*. This is a good example of dynamic organization.

—Ben Shahn makes a strong statement in *The Red Staircase*. (p. 104) What does the staircase mean? What is behind the wall?

TRY THIS

—Choose a poem (try one by e. e. cummings or Dylan Thomas). Write or letter it in a style that interprets its meaning. Be sure to keep the same word placement. This is part of the shape that the poet gives his work. Use color expressively.

—Make an imaginary insect — draw it or construct it. Let it be ferocious, timid, hilarious. Go to science books to see the wonderful design of real insects.

—Design a sports car, using shapes that express function and speed.

—Find a photograph of a face. Cut it apart in shapes that intensify the expression. Separate them or shift them as you paste.

—Select a magazine photo of a person in action. Draw that same action, exaggerating to emphasize strength, speed, weariness, etc.

—Draw a weary bicycle, a sad sailboat, a nervous scissors.

43

ADVERTISEMENT Hypnotism

There's another kind of shape that is aiming to shape you. It slinks onto your TV screen, or leaps in; it drifts off into smoke. Then it becomes a voice that has a shape — smooth or husky or little-brotherish.

You meet it on every page of your magazine and along our city streets, on your buses — the shape of words, words that sell. They may be bold or hot or neon-flashing. Their shape is in their letter forms. Their shape is their meaning.

Advertising is shaping much of our daily living. It creates new necessities. It also forces better products. But the "everybody's doing it" approach that it uses, edges us into letting "everybody" do our deciding.

Watch for generalization, the over-statement, the faulty reasoning. You can find it in words, but it is more often in shapes, in the picture-message.

TRY THIS

— Cut out many "sell" captions from advertisements to develop your own statement on life, friendship, success.

— Cut letters for a word, designing them to express the word — fantastic, heavy, smooth.

— Design an advertisement. Decide on the approach you want to use.

— Plan a TV commercial.

— Do a one-word poster.

LOOK

— for shapes that shout their message

— for the "soft-sell" approach

— for sales appeal in store window displays

— for advertisements that use little or no copy; how is the message delivered?

LISTEN

— to the sound effects in commercials

— to their "pressure level"

— to the use of music to create an atmosphere for a product.

WHAT DO YOU THINK?

— Advertising design in art today really demands a "what if" approach. Look for examples of good design and "new" thinking in ads.

— Find the overstatement and generalization in ads. Look too for the understatement. Compare and discuss them.

— Compare the sales pitch in a 'teen magazine, a woman's magazine, a news magazine.

ADVERTISEMENT Jackie Gleason

As we live in this world of ours, we experience space. We push through crowds, or run in the wide-open country or perhaps in a playground. We know inside and outside, close and far, pressed in and free.

Our astronauts have brought back photographs to share their new "way out" experience of space.

What is space to the painter? Perspective? Yes, that is one answer. But there are others. Space is just as personal to the artist as color is. He 'speaks' through the *picture plane*, the flat surface of his material, and the *picture space;* that is, the illusion of moving into the picture.

The Egyptian artist, painting on walls of homes and tombs, kept the wall-feeling by dividing his picture plane geometrically. In these rectangles he could show a whole panorama of a man's estate. In the first painting on page 48, notice the top-side view of the water. In the second, notice the rows of workers—the grape pickers, the men treading the wine press, etc. The Egyptian artist kept this flatness in his figures, showing them in a composite view — profile, front view of shoulders, side view of legs and feet.

Persian miniatures, brilliant little paintings done to illustrate books, used space as if it really belongs to them. (p. 54) The horsemen fill the page with rhythm. None gets smaller; all stay right on the flat picture plane, building up on its surface.

Size is a powerful space tool. Early Christian painters used it with complete freedom. In this fresco of the Tower of Babel, compare the size of the tower, of the men on top of it,

and the man handing them bricks. Imagine this same scene done with "realistic" space.

In the Bayeux tapestry you can see the castle drawn as a frame around the people in it. Here you see inside and outside at the same time, with a happy freedom of size. This tapestry, which tells the story of the Norman conquest (the Battle of Hastings in 1066), was done shortly after the conquest as a victory memorial. Today it still hangs in a long horizontal strip around the wall of the Bayeux Cathedral in France.

All of these artists were expressing an *IDEA* (or concept) of space, using their picture space freely to tell us something.

The Renaissance painters turned from this *CONCEPTUAL* approach to a *VISUAL* one, presenting a scene exactly as it appears, making objects smaller in the distance. As *right* as this may seem to us, primitive peoples just do not see space that way. Those primitives who, for example, have never seen a movie have been found to be disturbed by buildings "getting larger" as the camera moves closer and by people "disappearing" off the side of the film. There are many ways of seeing. Theirs is in relation to what they *know* (conceptual).

But with the Renaissance artists began painting what they *saw*, overlapping forms, reducing size, suggesting distant *picture space* with a *horizon line*. Giotto (who was a 14th century painter from Florence, Italy), began this with paintings like his *Deposition of Christ.* (p. 93) Notice the roundness of his figures. But his back-

DE CHIRICO The Anguish of Depart

Korean Painting "Study of Bric-A-Bra

FONTANA Concetto Speziale Atte

ground is still quite limited. Later painters became fascinated with *perspective* and built architectural forms into their paintings to show depth.

By the 17th century, Baroque artists were painting ceilings to give the illusion of breaking through to a vision of the sky.

Our perspective methods make things smaller as they recede into the picture space. But this is not the only way. Oriental painters do just the opposite. Look at the Korean painting of people around a table. Here the forms get *larger* as they move back. From what angle does the Oriental artist seem to view his subject?

Space has a religious meaning to people of the East. Many of their paintings have only one branch of a tree cutting into emptiness. The effect is a quietness that is hard for us to understand. (See p. 87)

Surrealism suggests vast empty space too, but usually with a horizon line that 'moves you far into a mysterious distance. Long shadows and tiny distant objects add to the mystery. Look at *Anguish of Departure* by De Chirico.

And today? Op artist Bridget Riley draws shapes that make the canvas appear bent. (See p. 10)

With new kinds of paint, artists are giving an *actual* depth by applying thick layers. They are *cutting* the canvas. Their colors "jump" right off. The door to space is wide open.

LOOK

—at a building from the opposite corner

—at a box from above it, below it, from all around it

—at the horizon line

—down a narrow street

—at the space in an elevator.

FEEL

—the space in a department store

—the wind out in the open

—the heaviness of a humid day.

WHAT DO YOU THINK?

A teacher told a little boy to look into the distance and see how the sky and ground come together at the horizon. He said, "But I was there and they don't." Can they both be right?

—The weightlessness of the astronauts suggests another opening for the artist. It is captured by Chagall's floating couple in *Lovers over the City, 1919* on page 103.

—Look at El Greco's *View of Toledo* (p. 52). Compare it to the photograph of the same city. What liberties did the artist take in composing his picture space?

TRY THIS

—Use the Egyptian method of space division to make a mural of the life of a teenager. Keep the flatness of figures. Make up picture-words to tell the story in some spaces.

—With freedom of size

and of inside-outside relationships, illustrate a poem or literary work from your English class.

—Try a *fun* variation on size. Do a collage combining parts of photographs to make an impossible situation.

—Do a contour line drawing of the school corridor, a staircase, a busy corner of the room, an open cabinet, or your classmates sitting around a table or at desks. Follow the angle of the edges as you see them. You will then have a perspective drawing without vanishing points.

—Draw a stack of boxes from above them and then from eye level.

—Find a magazine photograph of buildings in strong perspective. Overlay dry-marker lines to pick out the receding lines.

EGYPTIAN Wall Paintings ▶

ROMANESQUE Tower of Babel ▶

BAYEUX Tapestry ▶

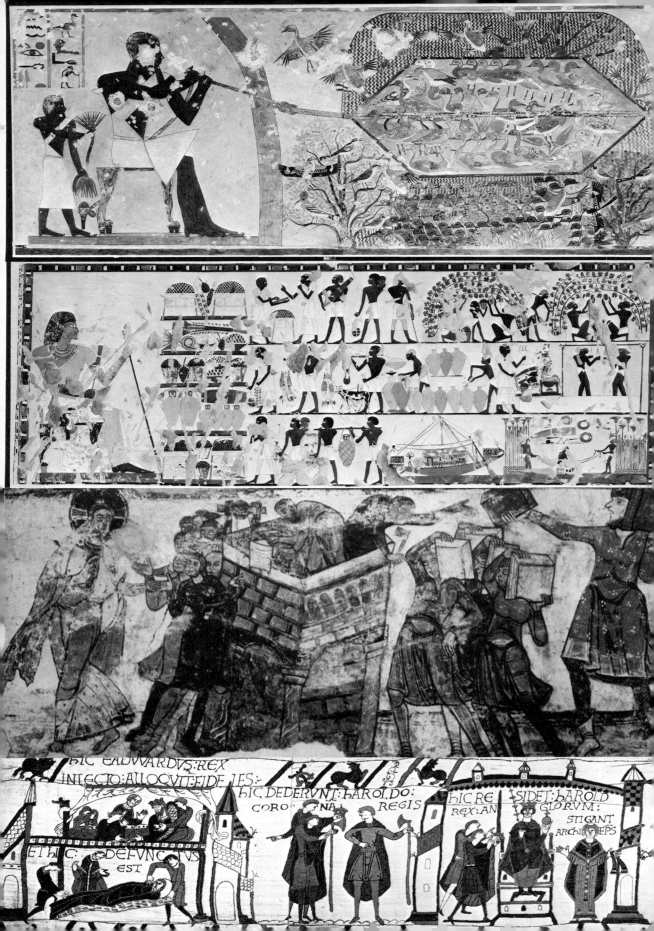

KLEE Puppet Show

CONGDON Nativity

KANDINSKY Improvisation No. 30

DAVID, G. Rest On The Flight Into Egypt

PHOTOGRAPH City of Toledo, Spain

EL GRECO View of Toledo

MARIN Singer Building

BYZANTINE Empress Theodora
MONDRIAN Broadway Boogie Woogie

PERSIAN Hunting Scer

54

MATISSE Still Life: Apples on Pink Tablecloth

OLDENBURG Dual Hamburgers

KELLY Green, Blue, Red

CHRYSSA Analysis of the Letter B ▶

◀ LALIBERTE St. George and The Dragon

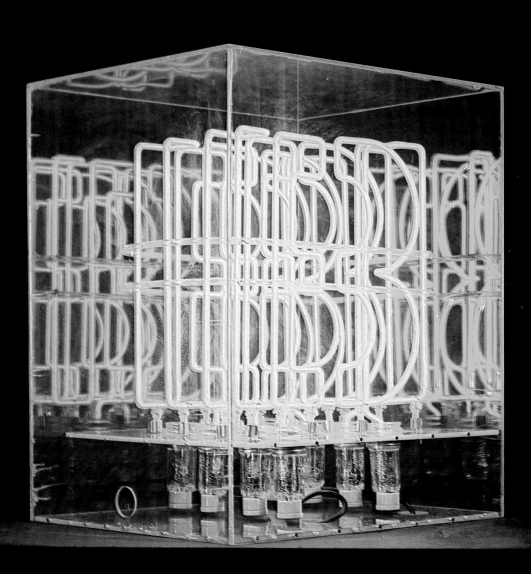

MONET The St. Lazare Railroad Station

CEZANNE Fruit And A Jug

BRAQUE Still Life: Le Jour

RYDER Toilers of the Sea

DUBUFFET The Cow with the Subtile Nose

VAN GOGH Sunflowers

ROTHKO Number 10

AFRICAN   Ancestor Statue

Cubists wanted to show many sides of a thing at once. Sculptors let you walk all around it, seeing new forms and new relationships at every step.

Marble and stone want heavy, solid shapes. Bronze or sheet metal can reach out, can rise up on a thin support, can wrap around space, can create open forms. Stone must start with a block and be carved into, but clay can be modeled or put together in slabs.

Wood grain follows the form of the log or block as it is carved, and adds its special rhythm to the sculptural form. But, as with all sculpture, it is the inner movement more than the surface details that gives unity and expression.

Sculpture has been with us right from the beginning. Prehistoric man carved the shapes of bisons and other animals into animal horns and bones, as well as into stones.

In this African ancestor statue, the roundness of the ivory tusk is kept in the carved form.

Science has opened new worlds to today's sculptors. You can find plastics, metals, concrete, even neon lights in their sculptures. Some look to the junk yards and put together the shapes of smashed fenders and gears. Others are combining metal forms large enough for you to walk through.

Kinetic, or moving sculpture is another of today's art forms. Its movement can even be programmed on a computer. Jean Tinguely's *Self-Destroying Machine* actually *did* destroy itself.

Open your eyes for new forms. Newspaper and magazine articles will keep you up to date.

MOORE   Reclining Figure (stone)

MOORE   Reclining Figure (bronze)

ARMITAGE   Family Going for a Walk

CALDER Mobile

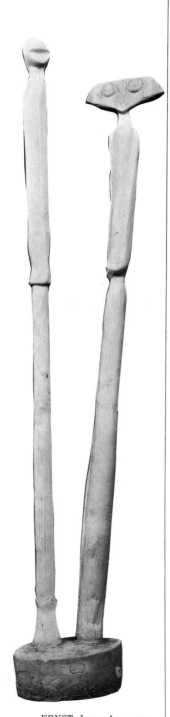

ARP Growth

ERNST Lunar Asparagus

BRANCUSI King of Kings

GIACOMETTI Walking Man

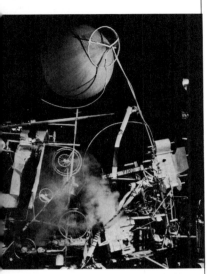

TINGUELY Self-Destroying Machine

LOOK

—at the structure of a green pepper cut in half

—at the motor of a car

—at statues in a park

—at a crumpled piece of paper from all sides

—at shapes in a tree trunk

—at the breast bone of a turkey.

FEEL

—the shape of a stone, of a shell

—the contours of your face.

WHAT DO YOU THINK?

—Henry Moore's reclining figure has hollow spaces that lead your eye to the other side. Can you get an idea of hills and caves from his figures? Do you think he intends this?

—The color of sculpture comes from its lights and shadows. Notice how sharp forms create blacks, but rounded forms pick up softer shadows. Look for lights and shadows in Moore's figure. Notice the difference in texture of his bronze and marble figures.

—Have you seen playground sculpture? Many playgrounds are being designed with abstract sculptural forms for children to climb on and through. Is sculpture meant to be felt? (But remember not to touch it in museums!)

—What does Kenneth Armitage's *Family Going for a Walk* express about the family through its bronze form?

—Compare Alberto Giacometti's bronze *Walking Man* to Hans Arp's marble *Growth*. Does the material determine the shape possibilities?

—Watch the movements of a dance. Or take poses expressive of emotions. Watch while one member of the class goes through the motion of throwing a ball, lifting a weight, doing some of your dance steps. Try sketching the movement as you watch it.

TRY THIS

—Carve a block of plaster and vermiculite, foam glass, paraffin, or balsa wood. Try to make planes, create shadow forms, make a movement flow around, or through the block. A modeling, or building-up process is very different from a carving, or cutting down approach.

—Use clay to model a figure that you can title *Joy, Fear, Anger,* or make an abstract interpretation of your dances. Use your fingers more than tools. What kinds of open *spaces* can you make with clay? Can you make a more open form than you can in wood?

—Construct an animal form with a continuous movement of wire. Let every wire line suggest action. You might work over this with strips of paper dipped in wallpaper paste to make planes connecting your wire lines. Leave some spaces open.

—Find pieces of wood or other materials. Assemble them into a construction. Do it as a model of a walk-through sculpture.

—Fold, cut, score, and bend a sheet of paper to make it into a 3-D form.

—Make a five or six-foot construction with cardboard boxes. Assemble them; attach them; cut openings. Paint planes, or use black and white photos on it to give another dimension.

—Can you design a sculptural form that moves? What materials can you use? Look at Alexander Calder's mobiles. These move as they hang. Build a kinetic sculpture on a base.

GREEK Parthenon

Picture yourself in the middle of Yankee Stadium, or a Gothic cathedral, or the thirty-second floor of a skyscraper. In the middle — because there is the place you need to be to understand architecture. Walls are important, but the *space* they enclose is what makes a house, or a church, or a shopping center.

From cave days on, man has been designing for living. Two factors are involved in shaping his ideas:

1. the function — what he will do in it.

2. the material he has — what kinds of space it can make.

When the Egyptians and the Greeks built their stone temples, they meant them to be shrines for their gods. The people never assembled inside. So the rows of columns that held up the roof in a simple post and lintel structure were no problem.

The Romans however needed buildings for their law-courts and meeting places, so they designed them with the arch, vault, and dome constructions. *The Pantheon*, a temple dedicated to all their gods, is a cylinder with a dome roof, needing no columns for support. Still using stone, they then could make larger interior spaces. The design of their basilica, a court house or community center, was used later as the design of Christian churches, because there, too, space was needed for assembly. The basilica form uses arches and columns to support a center aisle and side aisles.

But these structures required very thick walls and buttresses, or added thickness, to support the thrust, or downward pressure of the roof span. The Gothic cathedral was a tremendous solution to this problem. Setting the buttresses like pillars away from the wall, the Gothic designers found they could support it better by an arm reaching over to it, than by a thickness next to it.

These supporting arms, called flying buttresses, made it possible to build the walls of the Gothic cathedrals higher and thinner. Immense sections could be used for stained glass windows, in contrast to the small, heavy windows of the Romanesque style of architecture. Throughout the years, Gothic cathedrals were built higher and higher, expressing a reaching to God in their soaring spaces.

The Renaissance, with its return to the quiet horizontal movement of the Greek period, began to build wider and lower structures, with Greek columns and pediments, often only for decoration. This style was suitable for multi-room mansions and palaces.

When America began to build, it was a time of *eclecticism*, or revivals of past styles. So our capitols are often Greek and Roman temples; our churches are Gothic cathedrals. America is dotted with Swiss chalets, medieval castles and English cottages. The Victorian period, in the late 19th century, put all of these together in elaborate profusions of peaks and turrets and arches, carved columns, and balustrades. Interiors, though they had high ceilings, gave a closed-in space effect, filled as they were with elaborate furniture and heavy draperies. It was certainly an age of splendor. Today we call it "gingerbread".

ROMANESQUE Tournou Interior
GOTHIC Rouen Interior
GOTHIC Chartres Buttresses

GOTHIC   Rouen Buttresses

LOOK

—for arches, domes, columns in the buildings around you

—for Victorian "gingerbread"

—at the beauty of old trees around a house, down a street

—for old doorways and stairs.

WHAT DO YOU THINK?

—Find out when some of the buildings in your neighborhood, or your city, were built. Gather pictures of America's various styles and identify them.

—As with all art, architectural form 'speaks'. What does the eclectic say about America's beginning? Look also for examples of colonial and pioneer homes. These speak of early America, too.

—Find examples of architecture of other lands and discuss the form in relation to the materials and the personality of the country.

TRY THIS

—Do contour line sketches of old houses. Get the details of their decoration in your sketches.

—Use heavy corrugated paper to built a Romanesque wall with an attached buttress and a Gothic wall with a flying buttress.

—Do a pattern design with a repeat of one of the motifs of the past — the pointed Gothic arch, the Greek column and capital, the Roman round arch, the onion-shaped dome of the East. Find others.

The Ndebele house is living space today for people in a small African village. Mud walls take a circular form to support a thatched roof over one large room. The simplicity of the life of these people speaks out in this shape, and also in the painted and raked designs on the walls and the ground of its courtyard.

As their needs grew more complex, the people of past centuries worked for ever-larger forms, but always with heavy stone, brick, wood.

But in America today, as in most parts of the world, we have new needs and new materials to meet them. The Industrial Revolution started this — factories, then office buildings, then large apartment houses for all the workers. Life was no longer centered in little towns and farms.

Two important materials have met new needs: steel to build high and wide, and reinforced concrete to take the new shapes. Many other materials — glass, aluminum, plastics, laminated wood, all add to the possibilities for function and beauty.

The first factories were ugly, big boxes, cold and drab. They were eyesores, spoiling the living areas around them. Today, although we still have far too many of the old, new factories are being designed with beauty outside and inside, pleasant working areas, and forms that are an attractive part of a neighborhood.

Look for photographs of steel structures. Notice the design use of horizontal and vertical lines, masses and open spaces that are possible. Mies van der Rohe's buildings often have walls of glass with steel frames.

AFRICAN
Ndebele House

AFRICAN
Ndebele Gate

CORBUSIER
Ronchamp Church

WRIGHT
Guggenheim Museum

NERVI Detailed Sketch of Stadium

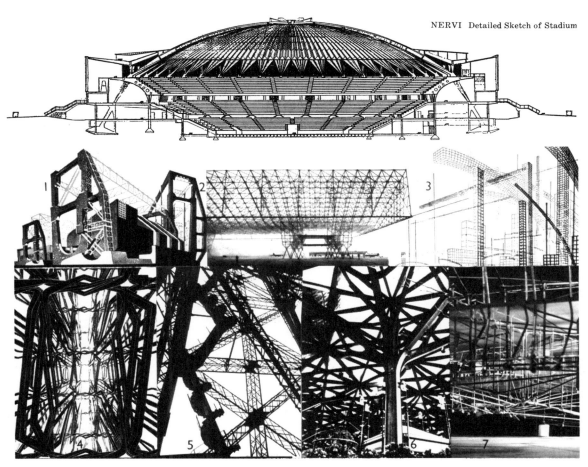

PETER COOK "Architecture: Action and Plan"

FULLER Inagamachi Golf Club, Tokyo

SAFDIE Habitat

Concrete is not new. The Romans used it over 2000 years ago, but they cast thick walls to keep them from cracking. Concrete has tremendous compressive, pressing-down strength but little tensile or bending strength. But now, with steel reinforcement, it has both kinds of strength. Thin shells of concrete can span spaces of 250 feet or more, without columns. Pier Luigi Nervi's stadium does this in a gleaming white network of fine lines.

What of today's designs for homes, for high-rise structures, for tri-level or row houses? Form derived from function opens many questions to the architect. How will people live in these spaces? Should a high-rise be a community building, with recreation and meeting areas? How can the architect provide light and air for so many?

Tri-level homes break down the old style of walls closing in rooms. In these homes, walls are fewer and often become only partitions, creating a free, flowing space. Often they join the inside and outside with glass walls and natural materials, such as stone and slate.

LOOK

—at the houses in your neighborhood

—at their roof shapes, porches, windows

—at the design of a shopping center

—for steel construction

—for fifteen other building materials.

WHAT DO YOU THINK?

—Many American cities have grown because of business and industry. They often show the results of poor planning. Find examples of this. What solutions to this problem are in effect today?

—Invite an architect to talk to the class about methods of using reinforced concrete or about city and community planning.

—Find photographs of as many different concrete forms as you can. Look at the Guggenheim Museum on page 71. Discuss the relation of forms such as this to their function.

—Compare the decoration in a Victorian house to that of a modern house. Discuss the difference between *applied* ornament that is carved in or added on, and *structural* ornament that is the direct result of the material or structure.

—Just as the eclectic period has something to say about the America of the 1800's, so our contemporary forms express today. How has America changed? What do today's forms say about it?

—In the designs of its new Embassy buildings throughout the world, the United States is incorporating the spirit and materials of each country. Find pictures of our Embassies in Ireland, England, India, Japan, and several more. Compare them to the style of the country. Is this eclectic?

—Frank Lloyd Wright was one of America's greatest architects. His organic style, "growing out of the ground" and relating to natural materials, has influenced some of today's architecture. Find more examples of his work.

—Find information about at least one of these great architects of today: LeCorbusier, Eero Saarinen, Edward Durell Stone, Mies Van der Rohe, Philip Johnson, Marcel Breuer. Look in architectural magazines for more.

—Take one aspect of interior design — light, space, material, relation to people — and find several different examples to report on.

TRY THIS

—Design a home that you would like to have. Make a floor plan and a cardboard scale model of it. Give thought to the kinds of rooms you need, the flow of movement through the house. Decide on the kinds of materials you could use for function and for beauty.

—Collect photographs of as many high steel constructions as you can. Cut out just the buildings, with their horizontal or vertical design. Combine them into a good design, *Rhythm of the City.*

INDIAN (N.W.) Frog Design

ROMANESQUE
Catalon Madonna and Child

GOTHIC
Chartres Cathedral (Detail)

Art is and has always been *peoplish,* touching the pulse of people and expressing the deep rhythms of their lives. One of the deepest has been religion, man's expression of worship. His ideas of this worship and of God have been many.

His buildings show this difference. Compare this Mayan pyramid with the Greek Parthenon and the Christian churches shown in Unit 21. Since the Mayans worshipped the sun, their ceremonies were performed in the open on a high place. So a pyramid, solid, *setting up* a place rather than *enclosing it,* was built.

The Mohammedans developed minarets — tall, slender prayer towers from which the priest called out often through the day to remind all to praise Allah.

Most expressions of religious ideas have taken a symbolic form. Fear is evident in the design of African masks, fetishes, and ancestor statues that were used in ceremonies to appease an awesome power. Their totem animals, as well as the totem poles of our Indians of the Northwest, are symbols of tribal protectors from supernatural powers. The Kwakiutl frog design is one of these.

The Buddha figure of the Orient symbolizes utter peace attained after the struggles of life. Its form is erect and motionless.

In the early centuries of Christanity, the image of Christ in Glory was painted most often, using strong lines in symbols of eternity and power. This same, controlled dynamism comes through in a Madonna and Child of the Spanish Catalon style, and in the long, regal figures from Chartres cathedral.

The Gothic period turned more to the presentation of the humanness of Christ. Their figures are more relaxed, and often smiling.

The Renaissance, interested in Greek idealism, put symbolic form aside for physical beauty. The detail of the Botticelli Madonna is almost identical to his Venus. (p. 74)

In strong contrast, Judaism and Mohammedanism have rarely used representation. Notice the abstract design on this prayer tower.

And today? Many churches are being designed around the altar, bringing the people together in close relation to it. New materials make new shapes possible. No more blocking columns are necessary. Light and

MOHAMMEDAN Minaret (Detail)

MOORE Madonna and Child

simplicity are keynotes. This same joy and light are the key to William Congdon's *Nativity*. (p. 50). A return to symbol in this, and in Moore's *Madonna and Child* and Rattner's *Descent from the Cross* (p. 104) is a mark of today's religious art.

LOOK

—at shapes of churches and bell towers, of modern synagogues and Quaker meeting houses

—for animals used as religious symbols — the lion, eagle, falcon, cat, lamb, ox . . .

—for many kinds of crosses

—for plants in religious symbols.

LISTEN

—to a Gregorian plainchant "Alleluia" and compare its form to a Romanesque painting. Plainchant has no set pattern of meter; its rhythm grows from the meaning of the words.

—to Haydn's *Creation*. Compare it to Michelangelo's Sistine chapel ceiling—its movement, color . . .

—to Stravinsky's *Symphony of Psalms*. Listen for the contemporary use of *dissonance* (very close notes played together).

WHAT DO YOU THINK?

—Find out more about one of the many forms of religious expression. Show how its form expresses the key ideas and beliefs.

—Some forms of religious expression remained exactly the same for centuries — the Egyptian, the Byzantine (Eastern Christian), the Buddhist. Why has the Western form of Christian art changed so much through the centuries? Does this parallel the change in society and way of living of the West?

—Discuss with the pastor or rabbi of a neighborhood church or synagogue its style and shape in relation to the form of worship.

—Do you think that a religious image combined with a planter is good design and solid religious expression?

—Compare the Catalon Madonna to some of today's Christmas cards. Which seems to be the stronger idea?

TRY THIS

—Make a well-designed display contrasting forms found in religious art.

BOTTICELLI
Madonna With Pomegranate
(Detail)

BOTTICELLI The Birth of Venus
(Detail)

MAYAN Pyramid at Chichen

ARONSON Menorah

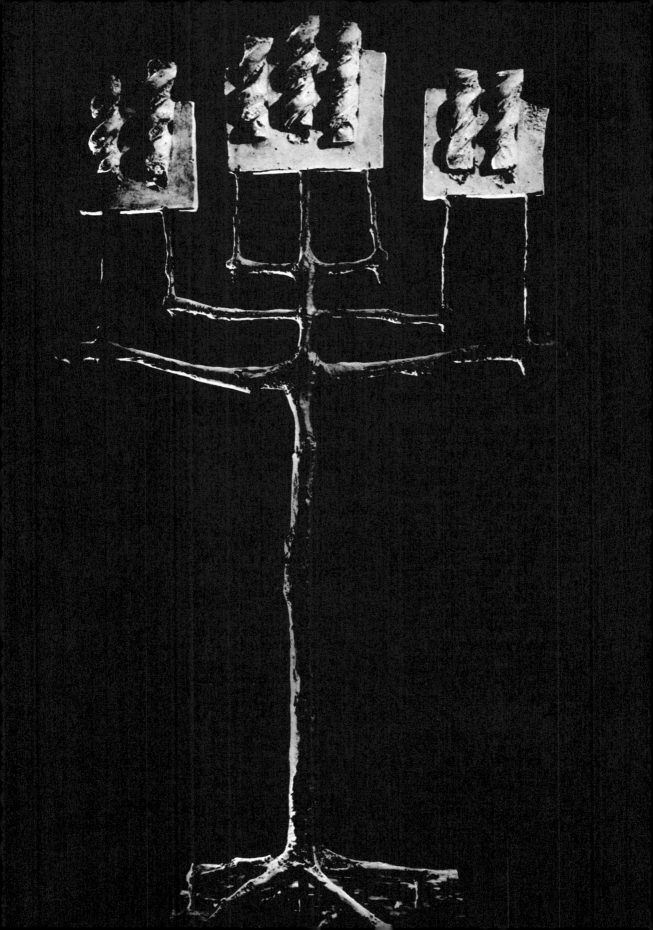

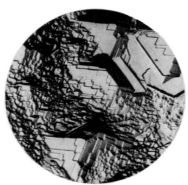

Magnified Oxide Scale on Iron

Look through just one eye. Notice how it limits your vision in breadth and in dimension. It is like looking at an ordinary photograph, and then seeing one in a stereoptic viewer.

Science and art are like your two eyes. Both are needed for a vision of the world in depth. Science and art have always looked at the same world; they look today through the same microscope, or prism, or telescope. The artist keeps alive in the scientist the sense of wonder that balances his measuring with marveling. The scientist opens for the artist new, fantastic aspects of the order and beauty of our world.

Science perfects new discoveries and the artist uses new materials and processes. The same adventurous imagination is necessary for both.

In medieval and even Renaissance times, artists and scientists were concerned with the world we see around us. Today, seeing the beauty of color and structure in a 1/25,000 inch crystal, or in a huge star 6 x 6 trillion miles away, is it any wonder that the "hill and house and tree" are no longer the artist's whole concern? Together with the scientist, the artist discovers abstract form, color, and their relationships; he for their beauty, the scientist for their function.

Science and art are more than just two ways of seeing. They are like two sides of a human balance scale. The scientist needs time for poetry, theater, music. The artist needs to keep in tune with the research of the scientist.

Very often they must learn each other's language.

LOOK

—for the microscopic shape of vitamin B

—for beauty in the functional forms of chemistry flasks

—for enlarged photos of cell structures.

WHAT DO YOU THINK?

—In a letter to the author of this book, Astronaut Captain Walter M. Schirra, Jr. said:

"I am concerned with this growing imbalance between the scientific and the artistic emphasis in our schools.

"Even with our high scientific emphasis, the arts are still with us. They are as important as they ever were, or they should be. I enjoy them to the fullest, I want to hear good music, or my favorite opera. I want to see a good play, or a good movie. I want my daughter to have this same privilege. I want her to have the opportunity to develop the

360° Panoramic Photo of Chicago Skyline

whole of herself in the fullest sense. I want her to have a well-rounded education and a well-rounded personality so that she may live harmoniously and cooperatively with people. And if this space age is creating a new 'monster' which would prevent these social attainments, then I should like to back down and take stock of where we are really going, education-wise."

What are your reactions to these comments?

TRY THIS

—Experiment with two pieces of polarized glass or plastic in a slide projector or a microscope. Place one under and one over a piece of cellophane or mica and move the top piece. Watch for unbelievable color changes.

Try this also with layers of transparent tape.

—Find out what use science is making of this new way of polarized seeing.

—Watch the pattern of ripples in water. Touch the water at one spot; then from two close points. Watch the intersecting of ripples. Physicists have learned valuable ways of measuring energy from this.

—Look for the shapes of analytic geometric equations — the parabola, ellipse, many others. There is beauty not only in the shape, but also in the mathematical order of the equations.

Magnified Snow Flake Crystals

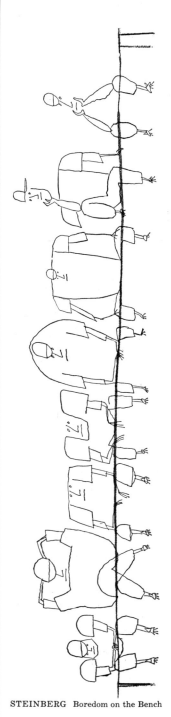

STEINBERG Boredom on the Bench

You've seen the artist designing buildings, painting and constructing, taking the world's great themes and making new statements of them. You've seen those who face us with the problems of today.

But don't miss the artist who helps us to keep our balance by making us laugh. What is the "stuff" of HUMOR? It is the unexpected, the odd, the way we react to a sudden situation, the "Linus blankets" that we all carry in one form or another. The artist zeroes in on all these human oddities and makes us laugh at ourselves.

Saul Steinberg, an American cartoonist, draws a conversation simply with lines. With a shape he describes the big business man saying "No", and the boredom of all bench-warming ball players.

Charles Schulz puts a mirror before each of us with his *Peanuts.*

Sometimes this humor becomes SATIRE, when the artist wants you to laugh *at,* not *with,* or when he means his humor to criticize the actions of political or social leaders. *Lil' Abner* is a current example; Alice (of the 19th century) met all of English society in her Wonderland through the looking glass.

In all these numerous drawings, the artist speaks his special language. He exaggerates. He uses the unexpected line, shape, color — or word or musical sound. Richard Armour uses rhyming couplets to give a staccato rhythm to his new view of a cow.

Cows
Do nothing but browse
And drowse
And now and then moo.

That's all they do.
Yet even while grazing
They aren't lazing.
Even while snacking
They aren't slacking.
If not illustrious
They are inner industrious,
Making milk with all their might.
With every bite.
Cream too,
With every chew.
I'd like it fine
Could I combine
In such measure
Business with pleasure.

Henri Toulouse-Lautrec, himself a dwarfed, crippled man, had a brand of humor all his own — revealing Paris café-goers, their pathetic pomp, their noise, and, very often, their deep-down emptiness.

LOOK

—through rose-colored glasses

—for exaggerated actions of children at play.

LISTEN

—to *Golliwog's Cake Walk* from Claude Debussy's *Children's Corner Suite.* Compare it to the prelude theme from Richard Wagner's *Tristan and Isolde;* see if you can hear how Debussy parodies Wagner's dramatic love song.

—to Richard Strauss' *Til Eulenspiegel.* This is program music telling the story of a mischievous boy. Listen for the 'sneering' tones, the pranks.

—to Franz-Joseph Haydn's *The Joke* from his Quartet in Eb Major Opus 33 #2. What devices does he use that are similar to those of the cartoonist or the comedian?

—to T.V. comedians Bill Cosby, Bob Newhart, Jonathan Winters, etc., and watch for gestures that create humor.

WHAT DO YOU THINK?

—Why does a cartoonist give his characters an exaggerated form? Compare styles of drawing in relation to the artist's ideas.

—Read James Thurber's *The Thurber Carnival*, or Ogden Nash's poetry. Try to get the *what* and the *why* of humor, the angle it takes in looking at life's problems. Look here too for understatement as well as exaggeration.

—Do you know people with "7-UP" dispositions? People who can turn the sun on when you are gloomy? There are many kinds of "artists".

TRY THIS

—Do a self-portrait in caricature, exaggerating prominent features or gestures. Use a line quality that you think goes with your personality.

—Design a comic character as a satire, or as a humorous situation

—Do continuous line drawings to caricature people running for a bus, being pushed in a crowd, learning to drive, getting flustered.

—Try a continuous line cartoon in wire, as Alexander Calder does in his *Cow*. (p. 24)

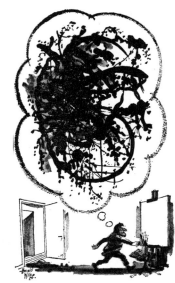

PUNCH Cartoon

SCHULZ Peanuts

STEINBERG No

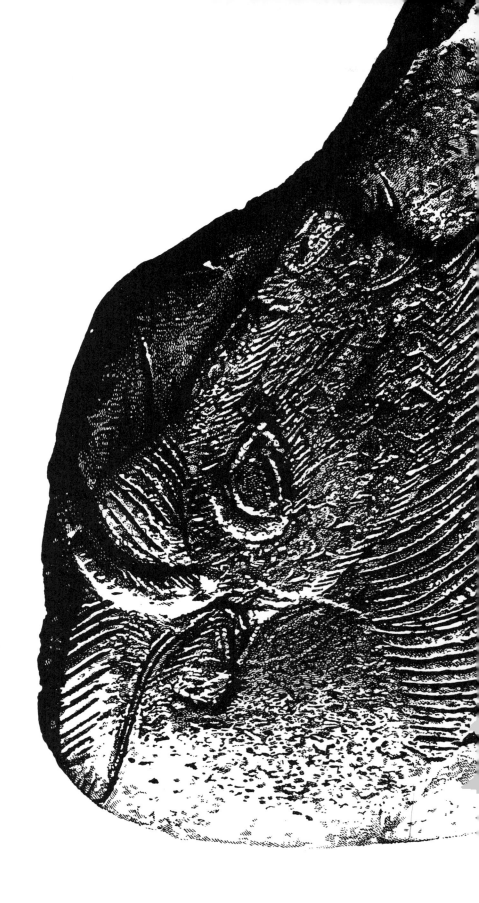

PREHISTORIC Carving of Bison on Reindeer Horn

What man has had to say about himself comes through visually from 25,-000 years ago until now. Look at him through this Folio, catch the rhythm of his ideas, of the pace of his life.

Prehistoric man's concern for survival shows in his sketchy stick images of himself, so weak in relation to a huge ten-foot bison. Yet even in a fight-for-life existence, his sensitivity as an artist could not be hidden. It was a wild imagination that saw a whole herd of reindeer in the skeleton of an eagle's wing. A few carved lines completed the picture.

The variety in art forms from then to today is greater than the selection in a supermarket. But a look at the powerful sketches made with the earth colors discovered by early man, should prove that *progress* can not be measured merely as development of skill.

There is no one standard, no one best form of art. The forms of art are as personal as people. Some are more sophisticated, some more direct, some wildly experimental, some emotional, some childlike in their simplicity.

'Read' man's art forms in the light of their times, their ideas, the materials they had to work with. Watch the speeding up of the pace of man's life from Egyptian times till now. It won't be hard to see why their art forms lasted 3000 years and ours today change almost overnight.

Happy journey through the ages!

SUMERIAN Worshipper

Take a jet journey with the speed of today into the pace of 3000 B.C. From the air, survey two centers:

Egypt, growing along the Nile like grapes on a vine, is secure within nature's protection — granite mountains, desert, Red Sea, Mediterranean.

Mesopotamia (now Iraq) also with rivers, the Tigris and Euphrates, as its "blood stream", stands unprotected in the midst of flat lands.

And from this stems much of the difference in their culture and their art.

Carving right into their mountains, the Egyptians made immense temples and tombs, honoring their pharaohs as gods. Colossal statues, many times life size, and massive columns speak the enduring power of this country.

The Egyptians were a cheerful, loving, family-style people. The wall paintings that decorated their homes and tombs tell in pictures and hieroglyphics their attitude toward life and death. They believed in an after-life and filled their tombs with all the necessities of that life — food, statues of servants, cosmetics, (all that women of today have and more), furniture, and even musical instruments. Their art tells all this in its static, peaceful style.

Governed by set rules, artists kept a geometric order and deliberate flatness that gives their painting excellent mural quality. Their huge columns, eight feet in diameter, include graceful designs, suggested by the lotus blossom and bunches of papyrus reeds.

Mesopotamia, in contrast, had a history of constant warfare. Until 1925 B.C. the Semites held this land. They were farmers, a peaceful, religious people. Notice the strange, intense quality of the figure of a Sumerian priest.

But from then on, the Assyrians, the Chaldeans, and then the Persians conquered Mesopotamia. Always needing to prove his power, the king was represented in a "propaganda-style" art.

While Egyptian sculptors used immense blocks of granite, the Mesopotamians worked in clay or on thin slabs of limestone. Their writing (cuneiform) developed from small wedge-shaped tools being pressed into the soft clay tablets.

Where the Egyptian art is stylized and secure, Mesopotamian art is naturalistic and agitated. Muscles are exaggerated. Notice the arms and legs of this winged being.

EGYPTIAN Columns

MESOPOTAMIAN Winged Being

GREEK   Head of Laocoon

ROMAN   Julius Caesar

ROMAN   The Colosseum

Already, by 700 B. C. the pace of history was quickening. Both Greece and Rome reached their peak and their fall within about 500 years, but they show two extremes of personality.

The grand ideal of Greece rose about 700 B. C., and had declined when Rome invaded Greece in 146 B. C. In contrast to the absolute rule of the Egyptian pharaoh-god, the Greeks developed democratic city-states. They were philosophers, athletes, poets, artisans.

Man was the highest point of their world. And in their zest for order and perfection, they brought their idea of Man into mathematical proportions. In statues of their gods and goddesses, whom they regarded as super-beings, they gradually reached their idea of a perfect human form.

You can see this idea developing in the coin representations of the goddess Athena. The early, or Archaic forms are stylized, having some of the stiffness of the Egyptian figure. But as the Classical style emerged, the features became very human in the Greek ideal — straight, strong nose; deep-set eyes; full mouth.

But this Classical idealism, with its quiet movement and strong features, was followed by a dynamic, but sometimes soft and pretty naturalism. The head of the priest Laocoon, from the late Hellenistic period, shows all the agony of an old man being strangled.

In their temples, the Greeks carried their logic into every measurement. The Parthenon (p. 68) expresses the Classic ideal in its calm perfection. We call this mathematical order the 'golden mean'.

When the Romans conquered Greece in 146 B. C., they began bringing Greek sculptors to Rome to beautify this city. The Romans were builders. They were engineers. They were statesmen and soldiers. But what to the Greek was an expression of an ideal, was to the Romans good material for decoration.

Their real interest in sculpture turned to portraits, sometimes idealized, but often realistic to the point of making death masks from which a portrait was cast.

Architecture and engineering were the arts of the Roman. His development of the arch, vault, and dome, as well as his invention of cement made much larger buildings possible. His roads, many still in use today, cut paths throughout all Europe. His aqueducts carried water to Roman cities throughout the Empire.

GREEK Coins

Turn off your transistor, take a deep breath, and slow down. This is one step toward understanding the mystery of Oriental art. But its real meaning reaches much deeper than on-the-surface quiet.

The Oriental painter will never make a quick sketch. He will rather sit for hours, even days, watching waves on the ocean or trees on a hill, absorbing the rhythm, the inner *aliveness* of the scene. Only when it is clear to him will he begin. Look at the sensitivity of ink brush strokes in the Japanese landscape, the beauty of understatement of space. The Chinese say that the idea is present even where the brush has not passed. Their paintings on silk catch this quality.

Even their animal sculpture catches the inner vitality of the animal, its form becomes, not an animal, but a rhythmic work of art.

The Hindu and Buddhist religions of the Orient have helped to create this contemplative spirit and the deep response to nature. Japanese haiku poetry, a special seventeen syllable form, is especially typical. Here is one by Shiki:

> *Long the summer day—*
> *patterns on*
> *the ocean sand—*
> *Our idle footprints.*

In the Near East too — in Persia (now named Iran) — this delicate, sensitive artistry takes the form of miniatures, which are brilliant paintings in books no larger than seven or eight inches. Exquisitely detailed and alive with rhythm, these miniatures harmonize perfectly with the brush style of Persian calligraphy (writing) on the pages of stories they illustrate. (p. 54)

CHINESE Fanged Tiger

INDIA (SOUTH) Seated Buddha

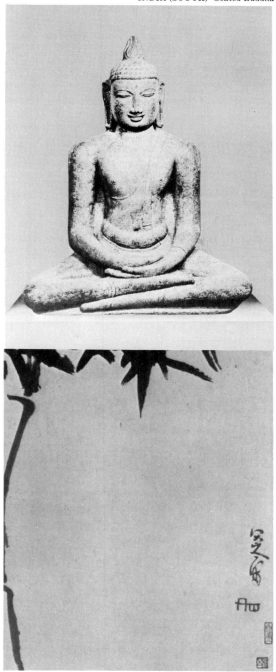

ORIENTAL Japanese Brush Drawing

JAPANESE Landscape

PERSIAN Calligraphy

CELTIC Cross

When Rome fell to Attila and his Huns in 476 A. D., the lights went out and the play went on in the dark, or so historians sometimes claim. But that is also where a seed begins to grow. The centuries following Rome's fall saw Europe as a huge mixing bowl in which the culture of northern barbaric tribes merged with Mediterranean culture as well as the influences of Oriental trading.

Christianity grew and spread throughout Europe, its forms of art and architecture becoming a dynamic expression of this synthesis. Intricate carving and expressionistic design of barbarian tribes mingled with Oriental color and symbolism, and the structural achievements of Rome.

In the East, around Constantinople, the Byzantine style had been developed even under the Roman emperors. They brought it to Ravenna and Venice, where its domes and mosaics still stand. Here are mosaics treated as mosaic — linear, stylized, stately forms, rich gold and blue symbolic backgrounds.

In the West, the Romanesque style reflects much more of the barbarian design. The powerful lines of its frescoes (painting done directly on fresh plaster) cover the inside walls of the churches. The rounded Roman arch and vigorous carving are its earmarks.

ROMANESQUE

Capital
Daniel In The Lion's Den
Enthroned Madonna and
Child

ARMENIAN Warrior

AND THE HARVEST WAS GOOD :31

GOTHIC Madonna and Child

GOTHIC Spire of Cathedral

As the 12th century moved along, Man was coming of age. From behind the castle walls of their feudal lords they came, building towns and developing their own skills. The Guilds, a medieval form of trade union, organized each group of workers — the masons, carpenters, stone carvers, shoemakers, bakers — and promoted skill and craftsmanship.

It was these builders who reached to the sky by means of the flying buttresses of the Gothic cathedrals. Especially in France, Germany, and Flanders, many individual towns began their cathedrals. Most of these took over 100 years to complete (four generations of families) during which many townsmen contributed their skill.

Man was recognizing himself. His Christianity focused on the saints and the life of Christ, in the wood and stone sculpture or stained glass of the cathedrals, and in his own trades. Painters worked on gold-covered boards with egg tempera (egg yolk used as the binder), and did exquisite paintings expressing their faith.

GOTHIC Carving (Toothache)

GOTHIC Carving (Pilgrim)

Turn the clock ahead just two centuries. The 14th century opened another "modern" age — towns had grown to cities. Trading and travel had produced many rich people from among the middle class. Europe was ready for all the newness that converged on it in this age of Humanism. Things happened fast!

The artist Giotto began painting really 3-D figures with life-like features instead of the stylized flat forms of the Byzantine and Romanesque. His frescoes fill the walls of many churches. This *Deposition of Christ* is from the Scrovegni Chapel in Padva, Italy. Then in the fifteenth century, the Flemish painter Jan van Eyck invented, or at least is credited for, oil painting. With this new medium, painters could blend tones and get richer colors than ever before.

Gutenberg's printing press, also in the fifteenth century, suddenly made learning available to many, rather than to the special few. Writings of the Greek and Roman philosophers, and the unearthing of their sculpture from the ruins of the temples heralded the beginning of the *Renaissance* — a rebirth of Classicism.

Sculptors began copying Greek statutes. Science and medicine became concerned with man's body. Michelangelo and DaVinci have left us many detailed sketches of the human body.

The Church was still the patron of the arts, but many wealthy people began commissioning portraits of themselves and their families. Artists, such as the Flemish Pieter Breughel, or the Dutch Jan Vermeer, painted the common people dancing, eating, working.

VERROCCHIO David

VERMEER Young Woman With A Water Jug

GIOTTO Deposition of Christ

MASACCIO The Tribute Money (Detail)

93

EMPIRE Chair

The hands of time move faster. The 17th and 18th centuries saw Europe in religious turmoil; they saw boundaries of the world widening with the colonization and Revolution in America, with new trade routes to the Orient.

And the artist caught the pulse of his time.

The quiet, classical forms of the Renaissance gave way to twisted columns, high domed ceilings, curves, diagonals, dramatic lights and shadows — *Baroque*. In El Greco's flame shapes and intense compositions, Baroque reaches perfection.

France, during the rule of Louis XIV, XV and XVI, reached another extreme — of the delicate, frivolous, extravagant. The Palace at Versailles was in sharp contrast to the poverty of most of France. The court painters closed one eye to the lot of common people and painted only the gaiety of royal pastimes. Fragonard's *Swing* is a good example. We call this style *Rococo*.

When the guillotine of the French Revolution fell in 1789, a new form of art spoke for it. We call it *Neo-Classical* — it really was Neo-Stoic — going back to the Greek Stoics who suffered unflinchingly. The sharp, precise style was the exact opposite of the soft blurriness of the Rococo. Jacques David's *The Death of Socrates* recalls the Stoic courage of the Greek Philosopher.

DAVID, J. The Death of Socrates

BAROQUE German Pulpit

FRAGONARD
The Swing

EL GRECO
The Annunciation

COROT   Le Dome Florentin

Like a chain of firecrackers, Napoleon's rise and fall triggered still greater change.

In the 1800's, Morocco set off another spark — French soldiers, fighting there, found an exotic new world of lion hunts and sword battles and blazing deserts. Eugène Delacroix's *Lion Hunt* shows the Romanticist at his height —painting far-away excitement with brilliant color and intense brush strokes.

Spain, suffering under a blundering king, revolted. Goya's harsh *Realism* spoke for it, painting ugliness and suffering mercilessly.

Honoré Daumier's *Uprising* brings this *Realism* into the French scene. He saw the first results of the Industrial Revolution, and recorded it in newspaper cartoons as well as in paintings.

Even the dream-perfect landscapes that formed Renaissance backgrounds felt the influence of Realism. Painters like Camille Corot, Jean Francois Millet, Charles Daubigny began painting nature as they actually saw it.

Today's world had begun.

GOYA   The Executions of May 3, 1808

DAUMIER   The Uprising
DELACROIX   The Lion Hunt

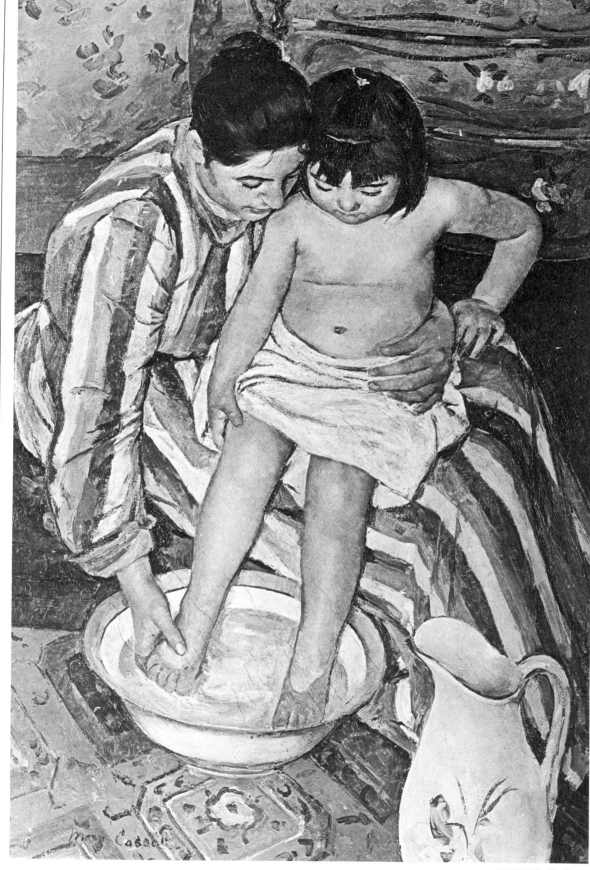

CASSATT The Bath

Rugged realism had led painters outside for a real look. With the findings of physicists about light rays and color to spur them on, they saw nature through the atmosphere of the moment. And they stayed right out there and painted. *Impressionism* was born.

But the public of 1870 was not ready for this hazy, broken-color style. It was they who coined the name when they complained, "These are not paintings; they are only impressions."

Claude Monet, the leader of the group, went farthest of all of them. Gradually he put aside even the cathedrals and haystacks as subjects, and painted large canvasses of the water lilies on his pond — vast, beautiful blurs of blue, white, green, with sparkling dots of other vibrant colors.

One more sign of our present day fast approaching is seen in the two women painters who were counted among the ranks of the Impressionists — Berthe Morisot and an American, Mary Cassatt. Both used the fresh new colors, but kept more solid picture composition.

MORISOT   In the Dining Room

GAUGUIN Woman With Mango, 1892

Before Impressionism was ten years old, art took another turn and branched out in many directions. We call its leaders *Post-Impressionists* (after *Impressionism*).

—Paul Cézanne took the path of structure. With all the freshness of Monet, he began to solidify his forms. Using small brush strokes like building blocks, he reduced his rocks and mountains, trees and people to simple, modeled forms.

—Vincent Van Gogh's emotional intensity pointed him in still another direction. His brush strokes became nervous lines and tortured curves of landscapes that caught his own moods. *Expressionism* was on the scene.

—Paul Gauguin's direction led him to the island of Tahiti, and gave his paintings the rich tropical color and pattern of the South Seas.

—Henri Toulouse-Lautrec brought freedom of color and expressiveness of form into his paintings and pastel drawings of Parisian café life.

—Georges Seurat carried *Impressionism* to its scientific extreme in his pointillism.

The roads were open.

VAN GOGH Starry Night

People called them Fauves — wild beasts! Never had they seen such bold color. This was a far cry from quiet pictures with delicate shadows.

But the Fauves went right on exploring the dynamic possibilities opened to them. No longer were artists painting things or people. They realized they were painting pictures — new realities on the canvas, not copies of someone. This new thing could say more than a photographic likeness. It could catch personality or mood; it could be a powerful composition, just as music can be.

Henri Matisse led these "wild beasts". His *Still Life: Apples on a Pink Tablecloth* shows his daring use of color. (p. 55)

Though many painters shared this title of Fauves, each was unique. Georges Rouault painted with thick and strong black lines, as in *There are Tears in Things.* Many of his oil paintings glow with the luminous quality of stained glass.

From the Fauves until today, the art world has seen dozens of "isms" — *Futurism, Purism, Surrealism, Expressionism* among them. Edvard Munch belongs to this last group.

MUNCH   The Cry (Detail)

CHAGALL   Lovers Over The City, 1919

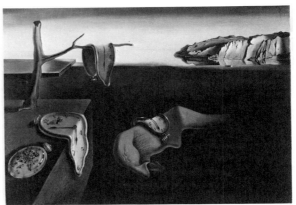

DALI   The Persistence of Memory

ROUAULT   There Are Tears in Things

It was a passion for freedom and a determination to build a homeland that led American colonists from Europe to ever-westward expansion across their new land. They had left behind the arts and theatres of Europe, and found little time at first to develop them here.

But many of these pioneers did find time for portraits and landscapes in a quaint but lively, primitive style. Their spirit is caught too in the simplicity of design in early American chairs and chests, weather vanes and patch quilts.

Some American painters, Benjamin West and others went back to Europe and picked up the sophisticated portrait style of England. Two of these, James McNeil Whistler and Mary Cassatt, lived in Paris and painted under the influence of the French Impressionists. Whistler was also influenced by Japanese painting.

But America was busy growing. Her artists often painted in a realistic style, capturing the America they saw. Winslow Homer's *Breezing Up* catches the playful spirit of the sea. He painted many fishing scenes and seascapes.

A group of painters in New York earned the title *Ash Can School* because of their choice of back yards and alleys and rugged city streets as subjects. Reginald Marsh's *Tattoo and Haircut* on page 23 is an example.

Look back through your book to see the many styles that make up our American art:

Albert Ryder's mystic forms of seascapes (p. 62)

John Marin's forceful watercolors (pp. 17 and 52)

PICKETT
Manchester Valley

SHAHN
The Red Stairway

RATTNER
Descent From The Cross

HOPPER
Nighthawks

HOMER
Breezing Up

EARLY AMERICAN   Bride's Box

Grant Wood's midwest mood (p. 22)

Lyonel Feininger's linear abstractions of buildings (p. 20)

Stuart Davis' sparkling designs (p. 18)

Mark Tobey's mysterious lines (p. 21)

Ben Shahn's haunting social comments (pp. 7 and 104)

Charles Burchfield's imaginative watercolors (p. 36)

Andrew Wyeth's fragile details (p. 34) and Ivan Albright's super-realism (p. 32)

Frank Stella's precision forms (p. 23)

The Abstract Expressionists, Op and Pop artists (pp. 10-12)

Sculptors Isamu Noguchi, Naum Gabo, and Theodore Roszak (p. 16)

Saul Steinberg's cartoons (pp. 25, 78 and 79)

Misch Kohn's woodcuts and Sister Mary Corita's serigraphs (p. 27)

Chryssa's neon designs (p. 59) and Mark Rothko's glowing color (p. 64)

Ellsworth Kelly's "hard-edge" painting (p. 58), William Congdon's joyous brush strokes (p. 50), Klaus Oldenburg's painted hamburgers (p. 58), and Norman Laliberté's rich color (pp. 56-57)

Kenneth Armitage's bronze sculpture (p. 65), Alexander Calder's mobiles (p. 67); and Jean Tinguely's kinetic forms (p. 67)

American architects Frank Lloyd Wright and Buckminster Fuller (pp. 70-71)

Find examples in current magazines and books of many more. America has come into its own in the arts.

From the 3000-year style of the Egyptians, we have moved to today, constantly accelerating. Where do we go from here?

This is an age which is questioning every rule of the past. The result is often a declaration of a new absolute. "Minimal art" tends to do this by rejecting every representational form. One of its leaders, Ad Reinhart, does all-black paintings with undertoned geometric divisions.

The strongest lesson of the past is that there is no *one* absolute. Art is personal, perceptive, often far ahead of its time. Art has always taken the materials of its times — today it moves toward the potential of light, automation, and synthetics, perhaps even "happenings".

The separation between the arts is dissolving. The computer is enlisted to program an art form in action, paintings combine with 3-D objects, taped sounds come from sculptured forms, mechanical constructions sway or whirl, ballet employs Pop scenery, lights flash as part of a painting. In all these ways the artist speaks of his time, often making strong statements about its social problems.

The artist has always been, and is still more today, the man who "thinks new" about the world that is his. Often today that new thought cannot be stated in the careful accuracy and display of technique used in past ages. It must be done in whatever form will state it best — from a plaster cast to a smashed fender to a Bob Dylan song about a lonely man. The artist speaks the struggles — and the unquenchable spirit — of man.

WARHOL
Campbell's Soup

RAUSCHENBERG
First Landing Jump

SEGAL
The Bus Driver

JOHNS Studio

INDIANA The American Dream, No. 1

INDEX

Art Education, Inc. takes great pleasure in extending its deep
thanks to all museum personnel, artists, galleries and other con-
tributors whose splendid cooperation so greatly aided in the
completion of this book. If an acknowledgement or credit has
been omitted inadvertently, we shall be most grateful to have
this called to our attention so that proper credit may be given
in subsequent editions.

JEAN MARY MORMAN *has been opening doors to enjoyment of the arts for eleven years to students at McAuley High School in Chicago, and also to adult groups both in lectures and on television. She received her M.F.A. degree from the University of Notre Dame, and, as an artist in her own right, has exhibited her sculpture and graphics in one-man shows and group exhibitions frequently.*

OLIVE L. RILEY *is Director of Art of the New York City Public Schools. She received her B.A. degree from Barnard College, and her M.A. degree from Teachers College, Columbia University. Miss Riley has authored and co-authored a number of art books for both intermediate and secondary students, which include* Art Appreciation; Exploring Art; Masks and Magic; Adventuring in Art; Your Art Heritage; *and* Understanding Art. *Her latest art book is due for Fall publication.*

MARY COLE EMERSON *is Director of Art of the Chicago Public Schools, as well as Editor of the national magazine* Arts and Activities. *She received her B.A. degree from Mundelein College, and her M.A. degree from the University of Illinois. Mrs. Emerson has taught art at every level from kindergarten through college. She has also served as Supervisor of Art and developed an effective program for the training of art teachers at the college level.*

ALBERT W. PORTER *is Supervisor of Art, Senior High Schools of the Los Angeles City Schools. He received his A.A. degree from Compton College, his B.A. degree from U.C.L.A., and his M.A. degree from California State College at Los Angeles. After teaching art in the Los Angeles City senior high schools as well as in adult education and courses for many years, he assumed his present position. Mr. Porter is also a professional artist, having had a number of one-man shows and group exhibitions in the Southern California area.*

NORMAN LALIBERTÉ *is one of America's most creative and versatile designers. He received his M.S. degree from the Illinois Institute of Technology and has taught at St. Mary's College, Notre Dame, the Rhode Island School of Design, and Newton College. Exhibitions of his banners, paintings and drawings have been held throughout the United States and Europe. He is co-author of the art books* Banners and Hangings, Wooden Images *and* Painting With Crayons.